Alcohol policies

World Health Organization
Regional Office for Europe
Copenhagen

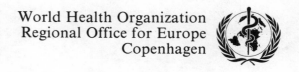

Alcohol policies

Edited by

Marcus Grant

Alcohol Education Centre
Institute of Psychiatry
London

WHO Regional Publications, European Series No. 18

ICP/MNH 027

ISBN 92 890 1109 2

PRINTED IN ENGLAND

85/6380—SB Datagraphics—5500

CONTENTS

Foreword

If we are serious about the goal of health for all by the year 2000, then we cannot afford to ignore alcohol-related problems. Throughout the European Region, and in many other parts of the world, rates of alcohol consumption and of alcohol-related problems are now so high that they give rise to considerable concern. Piecemeal attempts to deal with these problems seem to have resulted in rather inadequate conclusions. In an effort to find a more lasting solution, WHO has begun to give special emphasis to the development of national alcohol policies.

The concern of Member States to reduce alcohol-related problems has repeatedly found expression in resolutions of the World Health Assembly — in 1975 (WHA28.81), 1979 (WHA32.40) and 1983 (WHA36.12). Of particular relevance to the theme of this book, the technical discussions at the Thirty-fifth World Health Assembly in 1982 emphasized the need for Member States to develop comprehensive alcohol policies within the context of their own national health planning.

During the technical discussions in 1982 and the Thirty-sixth World Health Assembly in 1983, serious concern was expressed about the worldwide trend of increasing alcohol consumption and alcohol-related problems. Specific mention was made of the promotional drives that are increasing the consumption of alcohol, especially in countries and population groups in which its use was not previously widespread. In this connection, the effects of international marketing strategies on traditional value systems were highlighted and the question of the need for some form of regulation of the global alcohol trade for health reasons was raised. Issues of this kind imply that it is not only comprehensive national policies that are urgently needed but concerted international action as well.

Two important issues emerge from this call to action. First, alcohol-related problems are so serious, so widespread and so diverse that nothing less than a comprehensive national approach is likely to be able to make a real and lasting impact on them. Second, since alcohol-related problems certainly are health problems, the control of alcohol consumption becomes a legitimate and essential health concern. It is up to WHO to support Member States in their efforts to integrate alcohol policies into their national strategies to achieve health for all through primary health care.

It is also up to WHO to give a lead through its constitutional commitment to the coordination of international efforts both globally and regionally. This can be done through the active promotion of relevant activities, in its own programmes and in its relationships with other international agencies and its Member States.

This is, of course, a global concern and this book has important global implications. It takes its place in the long line of publications that have been produced by or in association with the WHO Regional Office for Europe. Its clear and practical suggestions of what governments can do to prevent alcohol-related problems through the design and implementation of national policies are a fitting development from Alcohol control policies in public health perspective *(published by the Finnish Foundation for Alcohol Studies in 1975)*, Alcohol, society and the state *(published by the Addiction Research Foundation in two volumes in 1981 and 1982)* and Alcohol-related medicosocial problems and their prevention *(published by the Regional Office in 1982)*. *The reduction of alcohol-related problems and the decrease in alcohol consumption are important targets within the European regional strategy for health for all by the year 2000. It is our hope that the results of the activities and the lessons learned in the European Region can be usefully adapted in other parts of the world.*

Many of the contributions to this book have been developed from working papers presented at a meeting on the control of alcohol consumption, organized in Paris in 1983 by the Regional Office. What is presented here is an integrated approach to the whole question of policy formulation. Past experiences are analysed and research priorities are assessed. A real attempt is made to suggest the logical sequence of stages in national policy development. The contribution made by economists is particularly important, since one of the many conclusions of this book is that a reasonable balance needs to be achieved between economic interests and public health interests.

But alcohol-related problems must not be viewed in isolation. They need to be seen as a consequence of particular lifestyles and of choices made both by individuals and by societies. What this book achieves is a sharpening of the focus on the prevention of alcohol-related problems without any loss of a wider view of health. It is concerned not only with promoting alcohol policies in a general sense, but with demonstrating that they are indeed practical, necessary and comprehensive. I very much hope that its suggestions can be studied and adapted by all those, throughout the world, who are interested in improving health. This book is, in a real sense, a plan for action and its success will be measured by the extent to which it is actually used in developing and implementing alcohol policies.

Leo A. Kaprio
WHO Regional Director for Europe

Establishing priorities for action

M. Grant

Alcohol-related problems are serious, widespread and show no signs of diminishing. Just how serious and widespread they are was acknowledged in resolution WHA36.12 of the Thirty-sixth World Health Assembly in 1983, which unequivocally ranked them among the world's major public health concerns. What is most alarming of all is that, as the worldwide trend in alcohol consumption continues to rise, there follow in its wake increases in a multitude of different alcohol-related problems that take their toll not only in countries that have traditionally experienced such problems but also, more and more often, in countries and population groups that have until recently seemed relatively immune. The need to tackle these problems is an urgent one. The World Health Assembly emphasized in that same resolution the necessity for countries to develop comprehensive national alcohol policies. In doing so, it followed the conclusions reached during the technical discussions the previous year, when it was recognized that such a flood of problems of so many different kinds is unlikely to be stemmed by any single strategy of intervention, no matter how effective.

An Agenda for the Future

Alcohol policies do not drop ready-made out of the sky. They have to be stimulated, developed and negotiated afresh for each country. They have to be sensitive to the history of the country, its culture and its drinking practices. They require imagination, tolerance, hard work and a sense of vision. They need to be prepared, formulated and promoted, taking into account a wide variety of legitimate but sometimes competing interests. All this is a formidable task, but a necessary one, if alcohol-related problems are really to be reduced in any worthwhile way.

Although each country needs to develop its own alcohol policy, designed to tackle its own problems in its own way, there are lessons that can be learned from the past and from the efforts other countries have made. The purpose of this book is to gather together some essential background information, to provide case studies of different kinds of approach and to set out the key steps, both nationally and internationally, that lead towards the development of effective alcohol policies.

This book has grown out of a meeting on the control of alcohol consumption, held in Paris in 1983 by the WHO Regional Office for Europe. It is important to emphasize, however, that in no sense is this merely a collection of the working papers presented at that meeting. To take account of the very active and forward-looking discussions that occurred there, the papers included here have all been very extensively revised, re-edited and, in some cases, completely rewritten. In addition, new material, not presented at the meeting, has been included. The result, it is to be hoped, is a book with the kind of coherence that will enable it to be used in a practical way in developing national alcohol policies. Much more, of course, needs to be done in this area. This book is not a set of comprehensive guidelines but it does, at least, establish an agenda for future action.

The Case for National Alcohol Policies

It is possible to see the world of alcohol problems as a battlefield. As far as one can see, from horizon to horizon, there are casualties. Some are already dead, some are dying, and others are still making desperate and pitiful efforts to save themselves. They are the casualties of the damage caused or exacerbated by excessive drinking, such as liver cirrhosis, cancer of the digestive tract and hosts of other physical diseases. They are the victims of road traffic accidents, of fires and of crimes. They are the victims of domestic violence, including child abuse. They are suicides. They suffer from anxiety, depression and a whole range of mental health problems. Despite the severity of the condition of these casualties, despite the apparent ubiquity of the battlefield, there seems little sign of any abatement in the hostilities. The great heaps of dead and dying mount daily higher.

There is, of course, concern. Faced with such carnage, it would be difficult to maintain indifference, either at a national or at an international level. But concern does not in itself presume effective action. It seems, indeed, that there has been some disagreement about how best to proceed in dealing with the costly and distressing problem of this global battlefield.

Various strategies have been suggested. There are, first, the *laissez-faire* free market economists whose view is that man is by nature a warlike animal; that the carnage is indeed distressing but that, given the right approach, it need not necessarily be quite so costly as seems inevitable at first sight. They point to the long history of the hostilities and to the indications that they are, if anything, increasing. In such circumstances, the elasticities of demand being favourable, they see worthwhile opportunities for the state to maximize revenue. If the battle is a fact of life, then it can be taxed to the hilt. A proportion of the revenue thus generated may have to go to financing services to alleviate the suffering of the casualties, but in aggregate terms, the world population problem being what it is, it is probably no bad thing to allow the scale of the battle to continue to escalate.

Such a view, of course, is incompatible with the public health perspective, incompatible with a sense of common humanity and incompatible,

2

certainly, with the aims of WHO. What, then, are the health options that are advanced as alternative strategic approaches? There are those who see the most urgent need as the improvement of the efficiency of the treatment systems. Confronted by the horrifying spectacle of all those casualties, they argue that the first priority must be the welfare of those already damaged. They plead for better hospitals, better accident and emergency units, better psychiatric care, more staff and new technology. Then there are those who, without wishing to ignore the plight of the present sufferers, believe that the priority must be the prevention of future suffering. There are two separate camps within this group. Supporters of one of these, arguing for health promotion, seek to persuade the combatants to lay down their arms or, at the very least, to use them for sporting purposes only. They are also anxious to counsel those who, though wounded, may yet recover if only they see the error of their ways and crawl away from the battlefield. The other camp, still in sympathy with the broad aim of prevention, have little faith in the likely effectiveness of these persuasive efforts, however eloquent or rational they may be. This camp holds the view that the only way to reduce the battle is to reduce the means with which to fight it. They argue for control policies that would restrict the number of cartridges issued daily to combatants, or limit the number of official munitions stores or, like the economists but with a different aim in mind, charge such a high fee for the privilege of fighting that few would be prepared to pay it.

None of these strategies is ridiculous. All have their advantages and would, in one way or another, lead to improvements in the present intolerable state of affairs represented by the alcohol problems battlefield. What is, however, immediately apparent is that, while *any* strategy might have *some* effect, all are partial. If, indeed, the level of casualties is to be reduced, then the economists, the treatment agencies, the health promoters and the control policy advocates all need to be brought together. Researchers also need to be persuaded to come out of their bullet-proof hides to help in forming a concerted and integrated approach to the development of a range of linked strategies that can be continuously evaluated. That, in essence, is what a national alcohol policy is all about.

Changing Patterns in Alcohol-related Problems

Since, as has been implied both in the opening sections of this chapter and by the wording of the resolution of the Thirty-sixth World Health Assembly, alcohol-related problems are essentially a global concern, it is important to understand the special relevance of the predominantly European perspective of this book. Its central thesis is that, in developing their own alcohol policies, countries can learn something from the successes and failures of those who have already attempted to make similar efforts. Purely in historical terms, the greatest wealth of experience in the development of alcohol policies has been within the European Region. It is, therefore, almost inevitable that this book should have to rely rather heavily on what is essentially European experience and European expertise. Since, however, it is a very mixed picture that emerges, with a range of different approaches to

3

different priorities, and with as many failures as successes, there is certainly no sense in which these European paradigms are being imposed on countries in other parts of the world. Indeed, what is offered in this book is offered in full recognition of the extent to which the lessons it contains are less inflexible rules than they are suggestions for future action derived from the struggles of the past.

Looking, however, at the factors that have had the most profound effect on alcohol-related problems in the European Region, there is no doubt that the most significant trend in the postwar period has been the same as in most of the rest of the world — namely, a general increase in aggregate alcohol consumption. An important point, in relation to this global trend, is that increases in aggregate consumption are associated with a growth in whichever problems are most common to each particular culture. Reporting in this book on international projects undertaken by or in collaboration with WHO, Mäkelä (Chapter 2) points out that in a very wide range of countries, including Zambia and Mexico and various European countries as well as two regions in North America (California and Ontario), it is adult males who still have by far the largest number of alcohol-related problems.

There are, nevertheless, some other groups of people who are currently of special concern in many countries. Foremost among them are women and young people. Clearly, while national alcohol policies have to be sensitive to their special needs, since they may well be particularly vulnerable to the problems that can result from increasing consumption, it is essential not to lose sight of the distribution of alcohol-related problems in the population as a whole. Within this wider context, the needs of groups, such as women and young people, and of particular regions within countries may well require health promotion or other approaches specifically designed to counter whatever influences are contributing to their particular problems.

Some other factors that may have substantial impact on the pattern of demand for alcoholic drinks and that may also influence the pattern of consequent problems have been identified as being of special current concern in the European Region. The first of these is unemployment. Although recent research seems to show that, perhaps because of increased social passivity and reduced spending power, the unemployed actually have fewer alcohol-related problems, there remains a powerful argument that suggests that their increasing sense of frustration and hopelessness could contribute to higher rates of social and health problems, including alcohol problems. What is perhaps more likely is that drinking, especially excessive drinking, by the unemployed could come to be seen by society as a different kind of social problem from the drinking of other sections of the community and therefore something that requires different kinds of social control.

Another area of concern is the possible influence of mass tourism. It has long been noted that the trend towards greater harmonization of drinking within the European Region has been associated with a process of addition rather than substitution of habits. Mass tourism may be playing some part in this process, both through its effect on tourists, in whom relaxed controls and lower prices can lead to increased consumption, and through its effect on the indigenous population, within which especially

4

impressionable subgroups such as young people may be prone to imitating the cosmopolitan drinking patterns of the tourists.

Although unemployment and mass tourism have been identified as issues of particular concern to countries in the European Region, this is certainly not to suggest that they are irrelevant to the rest of the world. On the contrary, both are factors that are coming to exercise increasing influence on the economies of many other countries as well. Other problems, too, have been recognized as having potential importance, although they have as yet been inadequately studied. Among these, attention needs to be paid to the drinking problems of migrant workers and the impact of population movements away from rural areas.

Costs and Benefits of Alcohol Consumption

It is clear from the preceding section how many alcohol-related problems have important economic dimensions. Indeed, one of the most striking features of alcohol studies during the early 1980s has been the increasing attention paid to alcohol economics. Among the many questions that have engaged the interest of researchers, none has greater relevance to the process of policy formulation than the estimation of alcohol-related costs and benefits. It is also, however, an area that is often bedevilled with imprecise analysis and exaggerated claims by those seeking, for whatever reason, to emphasize the importance of either the costs or the benefits of alcohol to society.

To be able to distinguish between legitimate efforts to make realistic cost–benefit estimates on the one hand and, on the other, doubtful justifications for partisan positions, it is important to recognize the basic economic principles that underlie this area of study. The first and most fundamental of these is the concept of the rational consumer. Since consuming goods provides satisfaction or utility to the consumer and since the rational consumer arranges his consumption so as to achieve maximum satisfaction, it can be inferred that people derive utility from drinking alcohol simply because they do it. This, of course, assumes that the consumer has all the information he requires to enable him to make a rational choice and also, given that information, that he will act in a rational way.

Both these assumptions have been questioned *(1)* in relation to alcohol. It can certainly be argued that, far from having perfect information, most drinkers are only very vaguely aware of the hazards of excessive consumption or of the levels of regular consumption that are associated with those hazards; nor are drinking choices always made on the basis of pure rationality. The pleasure people gain from activities such as skiing or motorcycle racing help them to discount more risks than can be accommodated under the rubric of rationality. In the case of alcohol, further confounding complications are introduced by its addictive nature.

The second basic economic concept that is linked to that of the rational consumer is economic efficiency. This does not merely refer to minimizing costs and maximizing profits, but is concerned with making as many people as possible as well off as possible, not just financially but also in terms of the

5

quality of their life. As such, its underlying principle is that of consumer sovereignty: that it is individual choices that matter most. The problem here is, of course, that individual benefits may involve social costs.

Thus, in assessing the efficiency in economic terms of any system or programme, it is necessary to be able to compute individual and social costs and benefits using a common unit of measurement. Here the economic concept of exchange value is used to be able to ascribe monetary values not only to goods that are regularly exchanged at specific market prices, but also more complex factors, such as human suffering and loss of life, that are not normally measured in cash terms.

The costs

Using these three basic concepts — the rational consumer, economic efficiency and exchange value — it is possible to approach the question of cost–benefit estimation. Many difficulties arise in determining precisely which costs need to be included and, as a result, empirical cost estimates often fail to take account of the extent to which alcohol-related problems overlap with other kinds of health and social problem. Since it is generally acknowledged that heavy drinkers impose disproportionate demands on health care systems, the prevalence of heavy drinkers needs to be clearly established so that the costs they incur can be disentangled from the costs incurred by moderate drinkers and non-drinkers. Equally, since heavy alcohol use seems to reduce life expectancy by about 10–12 years, its elimination (were that possible) would increase some health care costs, given that health service use is highest among the elderly.

Accepting these difficulties at face value, it can be seen that alcohol-related costs fall into two major categories. The first of these — production costs — is the value of the resources used to produce alcoholic drinks. It is, however, the second category — the social costs of alcohol consumption — that is generally the basis for cost–benefit estimations. Social costs are made up of both private and external costs, to both of which monetary values need to be ascribed. Granted that the more intangible the costs, the more difficult it will be to ascribe precise values, there is general agreement that four kinds of loss are quantifiable. These are:

— loss in total production due to alcohol-related problems;

— the commitment of health service resources to the treatment of people with alcohol-related problems;

— real losses to society from traffic and other accidents, fires and criminal acts in which alcohol is a factor; and

— expenditure on social welfare and education services for the prevention or alleviation of alcohol-related problems (2).

The benefits

Estimating the benefits of alcohol consumption is no less fraught with difficulties. In essence, from an economic perspective, the benefits of alcohol consumption are simply the satisfaction or utility that consumers derive

6

from it, which can be measured by their total expenditure on alcoholic drinks. Here again, the doubtful validity of the concept of the rational consumer detracts substantially from the usefulness of such an analysis.

What is clear, however, is that it is necessary to be very cautious about including either the creation of employment or the revenue gained from taxation as benefits of alcohol consumption. The one is contrary to the principle of economic efficiency, since it ignores the tendency of the use of resources to adapt to consumers' preferences rather than vice versa, and the second — taxation — merely represents a transfer payment that redistributes purchasing power without increasing consumption possibilities, either now or in the future.

What lies behind the problem of estimating the costs and benefits of alcohol consumption is also the reason why the topic is of such interest to those concerned with policy development. The range and diversity of alcohol-related problems and the difficulties of cost–benefit estimation, both point to the necessity of seeing alcohol as a special commodity that cannot simply be left to find its own level and in relation to which consumer sovereignty may therefore be far from the best principle. If this is the case, economics and public health seem to be pointing in the same general direction, namely towards achieving optimal levels of alcohol consumption, both for individuals and for society as a whole.

Balancing Economic Interests and Public Health Interests

While changes in the pattern of demand for alcoholic drinks are likely to have an impact on the range and severity of alcohol-related problems, so too are changes on the supply side. Detailed consideration of the international trade in alcoholic drinks reveals a pattern of continuing growth, especially in beer and spirits. Wine remains of particular importance, however, because of questions relating to the disposal of the substantial surpluses caused by overproduction. For many European countries, trade in alcoholic drinks represents an important percentage of gross national product. Recently, as domestic consumption in some of these countries has levelled off, so exports have become increasingly important.

The most spectacular rises in alcohol consumption are now taking place in countries in the developing world. It is precisely towards these countries that much export effort is directed, both in the form of the actual drinks themselves and in the form of the technology and expertise necessary for them to develop their own industrial capacity to produce alcohol. Marketing strategies, already the subject of some public health concern in Europe, are often relatively unrestricted in developing countries. In general, these changes in production and distribution structures are a new challenge to the development of international approaches to the optimization of supply, especially since the social and health implications of unfettered increases in consumption may not be appreciated in some countries.

It is, nevertheless, important to recognize how little is to be gained from confrontation with the alcoholic drinks industry. Just as it is unacceptable for alcohol to be released to the forces of unrestricted marketing, so it is

7

futile simply to heap blame on legitimate economic interests. There is, of course, a conflict between economic interests and public health interests, but it is not necessarily an irreconcilable conflict.

Its reconciliation depends on acknowledging that alcohol is a special commodity, both because of its potential adverse social and health consequences and because of its addictive nature. Although the current economic problems being faced by most countries may in some cases slow down the rate of increase in aggregate consumption, the range and severity of alcohol-related problems in virtually every country in the world are likely to remain at unacceptably high levels, unless concerted and sustained action is taken both nationally and internationally. The major task of any comprehensive national alcohol policy has to be to achieve a fair balance for that country between economic interests and public health interests.

References

1. **Leu, R.E.** What can economists contribute? *In:* Grant, M. et al., ed. *Economics and alcohol.* London, Croom Helm, 1983.
2. **Schifrin, L.G.** Societal costs of alcohol abuse in the United States: an updating. *In:* Grant, M. et al., ed. *Economics and alcohol.* London, Croom Helm, 1983.

Lessons from the postwar period

K. Mäkelä

This chapter draws together some of the main findings and implications for action of two major international collaborative research undertakings: the WHO project on community response to alcohol-related problems and the international study of alcohol control experiences (ISACE).

The Community Response Project

The main long-term aim of the community response project was to promote adequate responses to alcohol-related problems at local and national levels. The main purpose was dissected into a series of more limited but interlinked objectives, defined as follows:

— to describe and measure the extent and nature of drinking patterns and alcohol-related problems;

— to describe and measure responses to such problems;

— to explore factors contributing to alcohol-related problems and responses;

— to assess the strengths and weaknesses of existing responses and to make tentative proposals for desirable changes and methods of achieving them;

— to promote interest in the development of policies focused on the prevention and alleviation of alcohol-related problems.

The project was carried out as a series of comparative cases studies of selected communities in Zambia, Mexico and Scotland. Information was obtained using the following approaches:

— collation of existing background information;

— a general population sample survey;

— a survey of agents/agencies that provide services;

— studies of clients of community agencies

— observational studies.

The results of the first phase of the project have been summarized in a report[a] with detailed annexes on specific subprojects and on each of the study sites. The second phase of the project focused on monitoring changes in responses to alcohol-related problems in the communities included in the study and on disseminating the experiences of the project to other interested countries *(1)*.[b]

The International Study of Alcohol Control Experiences

The goals of ISACE were:

— to trace the historical development of alcohol control policy, its determinants and its effects on the levels and patterns of alcohol consumption in seven societies;

— to assess the potential influence of control policy on the consumption of alcohol and its adverse consequences.

To understand the social dynamics of the postwar increase in alcohol consumption and to study the control measures in their historical context, the project was carried out as a series of comparative case studies of seven societies, in California, Finland, Ireland, the Netherlands, Ontario, Poland and Switzerland. The results of the project are presented in two reports: the first report *(2)* is an international discussion of the postwar experiences (1950–1975) of the seven societies, and the second report *(3)* summarizes each of the seven case studies.

Comparative Case Studies

ISACE and the community response project both consist of comparative case studies based on a rich variety of information. An interest in the social dynamics of drinking and reactions to drinking is also common to both projects. ISACE deals with these dynamics mainly on the national level, whereas the particular strength of the community response project lies in the analysis of the local processes. The projects are further complementary to each other in one important respect. ISACE describes the social historical background and the structural determinants of the present situation, whereas the planners of the community response project had their eyes firmly fixed on a project oriented towards community action.

---

[a] *Report on monitoring responses to alcohol-related problems:* community response to alcohol-related problems, Phase I (unpublished WHO document MNH/83.17, 1982).

[b] *Report on monitoring responses to alcohol-related problems:* community response to alcohol-related problems, Phase II (unpublished WHO document MNH/83.18, 1983).

10

As noted by the WHO Regional Director for Europe in his foreword to the final ISACE report *(3)*, an analysis of the social dynamics and structural constraints of preventive policies is essential to the design of realistic measures to strengthen their impact. As other chapters in this publication focus more directly on the development of national policies on alcohol problems, the main emphasis here will be on the social and historical dynamics of drinking and drinking problems and on the interests and counter-interests related to prevention.

Alcohol Consumption, Production and Trade, 1950–1975

Consumption

By the middle of the nineteenth century, alcohol intake was at a high level in most countries in Europe and North America. At the turn of the century there was a decline in alcohol consumption that continued until the period between the two world wars. Between the Second World War and the 1970s, consumption increased in almost all countries providing reasonably accurate statistics, with some countries approaching the peak levels of the nineteenth century. The increase tended to be fastest in countries starting from a low level and as a consequence the gap between the highest and lowest consumption countries narrowed. Although the drink structure of consumption in different countries tended to converge, there remained strong national differences in the choice of type of alcoholic drink. The traditional drinks were not replaced by other drinks; the change was one of addition rather than substitution.

The fact that much consumption went unrecorded does not invalidate the statistical conclusions reached on the basis of recorded consumption. Home production was a declining factor in unrecorded consumption, despite the spread of wine-making at home in some places. Duty-free purchases of alcohol greatly expanded.

The relative importance of private drinking increased, particularly in countries where traditionally the proportion of public drinking had been high. The transformation of aggregate patterns of consumption can to some extent be attributed to the decline of the traditional drinking practices embedded in largely rural communities and other shrinking population groups. For the most part, however, changes in the drink composition reflected the addition of new drinking practices, sometimes associated with new drinking populations.

The postwar period witnessed the entry into the drinking population of new groups that earlier had been more or less excluded from drinking by social custom. Chief among these were women, teenagers and, in some countries, rural residents. Only exceptionally did the recruitment of new drinkers have any notable direct impact on overall consumption. Culturally, however, the decline in abstinence signified the dwindling of the temperance ethos. The relative shrinkage of the non-drinking group tended to be larger among men than among women. As there was a larger reservoir of non-drinking women, however, they predominate in absolute numbers among those who have recently entered the drinking population. The increase in female drinking is less important in its implications for alcohol problems among women than as an indication of changes in the social position of both women and drinking, particularly in cultures where drinking was previously a male prerogative and where drinking occasions had been insulated from daily routines.

With rising affluence, waning local traditions and the increased availability of commercially produced alcoholic drinks, the differences between urban and rural areas and between occupational groups are now less conspicuous than they used to be. Nevertheless, there are still wide variations in drinking and particularly in heavy drinking according to major social differentiations.

Not only were large groups of the population more or less secluded from drinking at the beginning of the 1950s, but much of the drinking also took place under special circumstances outside the normal flow of daily life. Over the last few decades the spectrum of drinking situations has greatly diversified. Drinking groups have become more heterogeneous in respect to sex and age, and drinking has become integrated with other social activities, especially those associated with leisure.

Particularly in countries where drinking traditionally took place on well defined and relatively rare occasions that were regarded as an opportunity for intoxication, the modal pattern has changed towards one in which more moderate quantities are drunk more often, but with less ceremony. There is considerable evidence, however, to indicate that the drinking of alcohol under these new conditions has not displaced the traditions of occasional heavy drinking.

None of the factors commonly put forward as explanations for drinking or problematic drinking, such as buying power, the amount of leisure, social misery or industrialization and urbanization, presents patterns of variation over time similar to those in alcohol consumption. The long waves of alcohol consumption are linked to complex historical processes and cannot be explained by simple factors or combinations of factors.

Production and trade
Between 1950 and 1975, there was a strong tendency towards concentration of the production of alcoholic drinks, particularly brewing and distilling, with the growing importance of international investments and conglomerates. The boundaries between the wine and spirits industries, in particular, became blurred and the alcoholic drink industry became interlinked with the catering and leisure industry generally. There was also a tendency towards a vertical integration of the production and distribution of alcoholic drinks, so that the distribution systems also merged into the catering, travel and leisure industries. Distribution outlets diversified markedly and there was a strong tendency towards concentration and chain formation.

The diversification of the distribution network meant that alcoholic drinks had a marginal bearing on the profitability of a growing number of economic activities. More generally, alcoholic drinks began to have a bearing on more and more varied interests and to affect, at least marginally, the economic conditions of increasingly bigger population groups. In summary, the status of alcohol as a special commodity, set apart from other commodities, was lowered and alcohol production and trade merged with those of other goods.

Alcohol-related Problems and Problem Management

Estimates of the prevalence of alcoholism yield divergent rankings between societies. This is an indication of the variability of alcohol problems and of the need to focus separately on specific problems.

In the 1950s important differences existed from country to country in the mixture of alcohol problems. In some societies the social and health consequences of specific drinking occasions were more important than in others, compared to the consequences for health of prolonged drinking. These differences were in part related to the degree to which alcohol problems were an immediate outgrowth of culturally accepted patterns of drinking rather than symptoms of clinically pathological drinking.

There were differences from country to country in the division of labour between the police, the health authorities and the social services in the management of alcohol problems, to some extent corresponding to the mixture of problems in each country.

Health problems
The overall picture of trends in alcohol-related health problems in the period 1950–1975 is one of substantial increase for most indicators in most of the societies for which data are available. The rise in alcohol consumption was accompanied by increases in the incidence of many health problems known to be caused by prolonged drinking, although the rate of increase varied from one disease and society to another. Because of the relatively long incubation period of many such ailments, their significance may be expected to increase in the future even if overall consumption stabilizes at its present level. This holds especially for societies that have experienced a rapid increase in consumption starting from a low baseline level.

The consequences for health of single drinking occasions are still quite important in comparison with the consequences of prolonged drinking. Societies have different characteristic mixtures of health problems related to drinking and there has been little sign of convergence over recent decades. In this period of increasing consumption, societies with a historic pattern of extreme drinking events and associated consequences — such as Finland and Poland, where substantial numbers of deaths from alcohol poisoning occur — have nevertheless experienced increases in both this type of consequence and in those effects of long-term drinking (such as cirrhosis).

Social problems
Over recent decades, actual changes in drinking styles, occasions and places, as well as shifts in attitude toward public drinking or drunkenness seem to have contributed to a depreciation of public drunkenness as a social problem. Tolerance of public drunkenness has increased, as indicated by more

13

liberal arrest practices and changes in legislation towards the decriminalization of public drunkenness. In the early 1970s, the growth in alcohol
consumption was accompanied, however, by increasing rates of public
drunkenness in countries such as Finland, Ireland and Poland where intoxication and aggressive drunken comportment are an outgrowth of culturally
accepted traditional patterns of drinking. At the other end of the continuum
are countries such as the Netherlands and Switzerland. The upward trend in
alcohol consumption since the 1960s has been particularly substantial in the
Netherlands but public drunkenness is not considered a serious problem and
the conviction rate is small and declining.

Drunken driving is an important exception to the trend towards non-
punitive interventions for alcohol problems. For drunken driving, the over-
riding trend has been to emphasize general deterrence through criminal
penalties and the withdrawal of convicted drivers' licences. Drunken driving
is exceptional in that in most countries it is an extension of more or less
accepted drinking patterns. In a larger sense, concern about alcohol and
traffic accidents has widened the definition of "problem drinkers" to more
than just public inebriates or those under care for alcohol problems. More
than for other drinking problems, drunken drivers are seen as representing
all social strata, both sexes and most adult age groups.

Changes in problem rate and mixture
The rate of increase in health problems related to prolonged drinking has
tended to be higher than the rate of increase in conflicts related to single
drinking occasions. Because of the differential rate of growth of various
types of drinking problem, variations among societies in the mixture of
problems have tended to diminish. Nevertheless, some cultural differences
persist. Along with the shifts in the mixture of problems, their distribution
within the population may have changed. Today, drinking problems are less
strictly confined to social outcasts and visibly deviant subgroups.

The available evidence supports the view that an increase in aggregate
consumption is accompanied by an increase in those alcohol problems that
are most characteristic of each culture. The mixture of problems in each
society varies according to its peculiar drinking habits and, in cross-sectional
comparisons, there are few positive relationships between consumption
level and the incidence of problems closely connected to specific patterns of
drinking. Nevertheless, looking at the historical experience in each culture,
the trend in problems characteristic of that culture is not unrelated to the
temporal variations in aggregate consumption.

Even in a given culture, the relationship between consumption level and
problems is by no means a simple one. First of all, cultural patterns of
drinking and drunken behaviour do change. In addition, many other factors
besides actual drinking behaviour determine the rate and seriousness of
alcohol problems.

Handling alcohol problems
Cultural perceptions of alcohol problems changed radically during the
period 1950–1975. Alcohol problems tended to be redefined as medical

14

problems. There was a growing awareness of alcohol as a causal factor in a number of physical ailments in addition to the classic ailments of cirrhosis and pancreatitis. Simultaneously, the role of drinking as a causal factor in social disturbance began to be seen as less prominent.

Among the trends in society's handling of alcohol problems, the most pervasive was the expansion of services for heavy drinkers, organized and financed under a medical rubric. The expansion of health services affected the division of labour in the management of alcohol problems among different authorities, causing a comparative reduction in the role of the police and the social services. The timing of the expansion of these services for alcohol problems was remarkably similar in different societies. The first modern wards or clinics specializing in alcoholism were founded in the 1940s and 1950s, but the quantitative expansion was most marked in the late 1960s and early 1970s. The expansion occurred along similar lines, seemingly irrespective of the baseline mixture of alcohol problems in each society. Common solutions were adopted for very different problems.

The locus of alcohol problems tended to shift from the bottle to the man — if alcohol problems were a matter of specific defective individuals, then there was no need to control the drinking of the majority who were not defective. In this way, the expansion of the treatment system may be seen as a kind of cultural alibi for the normalization of drinking and the relaxation of controls. Despite the expansion of alcohol-specific services, it is very clear from the community response project that specialized agencies are dealing with only a small fraction of the various alcohol-related problems confronted by the different agencies in the communities. Representatives of the non-specialized agencies are generally well aware of the contribution of drinking to their daily caseload.

Alcohol Control Policies, 1950–1975

Alcohol control here refers to the intervention by the state in the production, trade or purchase of alcoholic drinks, in whatever form or for whatever purpose. Thus, all control systems and actions related to alcohol are examined, not only those with the explicit aim of preventing alcohol-related problems. The definition does not, on the other hand, include all state actions regarding alcohol. Policies that deal with the management of alcohol-related problems directly, but that do not intervene in the market for alcoholic drinks, are not included in the definition.

Trends in alcohol control

In the areas of production, the control activities of the state have in some cases expanded since the Second World War, but they have lost much of their original purpose of limiting both private profit-making and the supply of alcoholic drinks. In general, the state continues to pursue restrictive policies in the non-commercial sector of the manufacture of alcoholic drinks, whereas the approach towards the commercial sector of the market has become less restrictive and more supportive. This support is in most

15

cases aimed at defending the domestic industries and, especially, domestic agriculture against foreign competition.

Agriculture

Many of the changes in alcohol control in the period 1950–1975 can only be understood against the restructuring of agriculture after the war. The declining agricultural population has meant that a smaller number of people now have access to the raw material for making wine, cider or spirits, either for marketing or for their own use. Also linked to the restructuring of agriculture is the tendency for the home production of spirits to decline.

The wine policy usually reflects the general problems of agricultural economy. International competition necessitates a constant improvement in the productivity and quality of the agricultural sector and the income level of the agricultural population must be secured. The course taken to solve these problems has been to improve the quality of wine, to impose restrictions on new plantations and to guarantee a demand for domestic wine by state purchases and by protecting the domestic market. The role of alcohol control as a protector of the domestic industry is not, however, restricted to wine. As tariff barriers are no longer so readily used, governments and national alcohol industries have become increasingly interested in other types of protective measure. For example, restrictions on advertising may be used for protection purposes. Without being advertised, foreign products have little chance of competing with well known domestic brands.

Taxation

In a number of countries, alcohol taxation has become lower, thus contributing to the lower prices that have encouraged consumption. This relaxed price and tax policy is related to changes in the tax structures of modern states. Whereas in the first part of this century the main source of public funds was excise duties, income tax has since become the main form of taxation. It is likely that, in the future, the tax burden will be placed increasingly on general consumption. The fiscal role of alcohol taxes has diminished, so that the fiscal argument in alcohol pricing has yielded to other considerations. One of the restraining influences in tax and price policy stems from inflation control. In contrast to general sales taxes, which are set on a percentage basis, alcohol taxation in most countries is based on excise duties that have to be adjusted by separate and politically visible decisions.

A further determinant of relaxed taxation and price policies is related to the structure of the industry. The increased political weight of big companies in the alcohol industry may have influenced alcohol taxation directly in their favour.

In addition, in the European Community countries, economic integration has lowered alcohol taxes in the new member countries where they have traditionally been at a higher level than in the original six. In the control of production, the scope and intensity of state involvement in the form of various kinds of regulation, subsidy and neoprotectionist ruling has tended to expand. In the area of distribution, on the other hand, old restrictions have been gradually lifted either by legislative reform, administrative decisions or simply by not adjusting old regulations to new circumstances. The wholesale structure of the entire food distribution industry experienced a remarkable change in the 1960s. Concentration and rationalization led to larger shops carrying a wide range of goods. These changes put pressure on the traditional licensing rules, originally geared to retail systems based on a large number of independent wholesalers and specialized retailers.

Tourism
Another important influence on distribution has been the growth of tourism. Mass tourism requires active marketing, highly developed organization, extensive planning and a wide array of services. The state has, in many cases, assumed a heavy share of the responsibility for carrying out these functions. A less restrictive licensing policy has often been justified on the basis of benefits to the tourist trade.

Outlets
In a number of societies, the number of both off- and on-premise outlets increased in the period 1950–1975. In societies where the number of outlets did not increase, or even declined, the capacity of the retail trade still generally grew as its structure changed. Small specialized shops tended to be superseded by discount stores and supermarkets almost everywhere, with the exception of societies where the retail trade is under state monopoly. Increased average unit size is also a characteristic of the restructuring of the on-premise trade. In addition, the postwar period saw a growing diversity of kinds of on-premise outlet even in the societies where their number declined. In some cases these changes required major legislative reforms. Elsewhere the expansion of the retail trade occurred by means of gradual minor reforms of the existing licensing laws. Finally, in some cases, the expansion of the retail trade took place independently of any state regulations.

The erosion of preventive concerns is further evidenced by trends in the myriad regulations imposed on sales practices. The main justifications for the regulations about the location and opening hours of retail outlets, legal drinking age, restaurant practices and restrictions of the right to sell alcohol to certain population groups, have not usually been economic, but almost always preventive. Over the last few decades the overall tendency has been to lift or weaken such restrictions.

Alcohol and the changing role of the welfare state
The preventive and fiscal aims that the alcohol control systems originally pursued have been overridden by other functions. The control of distribution and sales practices has been liberalized so that market forces now have a much stronger influence than when the alcohol control systems were founded. In the period 1950–1975, economic considerations overruled preventive concerns. This does not in itself explain, however, the absence or weakness of preventive arguments in debates about alcohol control policies.

A class problem
The alcohol question was an integral part of the working-class problems of the late nineteenth and early twentieth centuries. Alcohol control arrangements were an integral part of the state's attempt to deal with the working-class question and were supported by public temperance sentiments from both the perspective of the working class's own emancipation and the reformist perspective of the middle class.

In the period 1950–1975, the alcohol problem became less and less associated with the working class because of changes in the population structure and in lifestyles. Occupational and geographical mobility has meant that the lifestyles of different segments of the population are by now less distinct than they were some decades ago. The relationship between drinking problems and social class is no longer as strong as it used to be. Objectively, the social alcohol problem has been transformed from a public issue of class discipline into a problem of individual deviance or disease.

From control to treatment
The emphasis in dealing with the social alcohol problem has, as a whole, shifted away from alcohol control agencies to problem-handling agencies. A rapid expansion of treatment services for people injured by alcohol has taken place. In addition, social work agencies and the social security system have been charged with increasing responsibility for alcohol problems.

It is evident that the shift of the locus of alcohol problems from the bottle to the man and the simultaneous relaxation of traditional restrictions on availability are related to one another. Yet the shift of emphasis from control to treatment should not be seen solely as a reaction to the alcohol problem. More fundamental reasons for this development may be found in the changing role of the welfare state.

The weakening of preventive goals in alcohol control does not imply a reduction of state involvement in the alcohol sector. The state continues to exercise control in this area, often on an expanded scale. It is in the mode of state involvement that the change is seen. Alcohol may be subject to fewer regulations as a special commodity, but it is subject to a great deal more regulation simply by virtue of being a commodity. The alcohol control functions have become a minor but integral part of the state's increased economic functions.

The shift in emphasis from restrictive alcohol control to the treatment of individual problems is in harmony with the developments in the management of other types of social problem and deviance. Restrictive alcohol control could be seen as one aspect of the state's attempts to regulate the consumption and leisure patterns of the working class earlier in the century. Similar controls were placed on other aspects of private life and recreation (dancing and public amusements, gambling, etc.). Such regulations took various forms, ranging from total prohibition to educational efforts in the newly established public primary school system.

One of the most important developments in the political structure of most western states in the postwar period was the growing working-class voice in government, with concomitant policies that resulted, to varying degrees, in a convergence in the lifestyles of different classes and groups. The adoption of modern welfare schemes in the postwar period was accompanied by a decline in the kind of regimentation of lifestyles as is entailed by limitations on the availability of drink.

Thus, a number of important changes occurred in the role and tasks of the welfare state that have not only coincided with the developments in alcohol control but, in fact, made alcohol consumption less and less a separate target of state action. The fact that preventive alcohol control and problem-handling have been historical alternatives is therefore not a result of a simple homeostasis between the two. Rather it is the result of two different processes. On the one hand, social and health problems related to alcohol have become increasingly integrated into the major policies and programmes of the welfare state. On the other, the welfare state has become less concerned with regulating consumption and other aspects of private behaviour.

Drinking, Consequences and Control: Emergent Issues

The increase in alcohol consumption slowed down or levelled off in many instances in the 1970s and even some decreases are recorded. The economic difficulties experienced by most of the industrial world are obviously one explanation for this stabilization. In as much as economic growth will remain permanently slower for the rest of this century, increases in alcohol consumption will continue to fall off. On the other hand, the consumption levels reached by the end of 1975 should not be regarded as being in a state of spontaneous equilibrium. First of all, in a number of industrial and developing countries, the long wave of increasing alcohol consumption shows no signs of waning. Moreover, the process of automation may, by itself, have quite unpredictable effects on conditions of living and lifestyles, not to mention the impact of possible large-scale unemployment.

The mixture of problems is unlikely to change to any significant extent. The consequences of heavy drinking sessions will continue to be important, both from a public health perspective and from the perspective of the quality of social life. Given the surprising endurance of traditional patterns of drinking, cultural variation in the mixture of alcohol problems may be expected to remain significant.

Social policy
There are, however, many signs of changes in the social response to drinking problems. First of all, optimism about the treatment of alcoholism as a disease seems to be wearing off. Intellectual and scientific scepticism about intensive treatment programmes based on the classic concept of alcoholism as a disease has been accentuated by the fiscal crisis of the state. Because of the vast expansion in health expenditure over the last few decades, it was relatively easy to provide services geared to alcohol-related conditions. In the future, increased financial strain will mean that alcohol-related public health expenditure will be scrutinized.

In many fields of social policy, the allocation of welfare resources is beginning to be transferred from marginal groups and the elderly (i.e. non-productive groups) to those who are more likely to contribute to the national economy. In alcohol-related services, too, humanitarian and rehabilitative services benefiting unemployed and homeless alcoholics have recently tended to contract, at least in relative terms. By contrast, more public resources are being invested in alcoholism programmes to reduce the costs of drinking to industrial productivity. Industrial alcoholism programmes are very much in line with the overall trends in social control mentioned above — despite the medical vocabulary adopted by the programmes, they usually also imply a more continuous surveillance and control by the employers.

In view of the financial strains besetting the health and welfare sector it is doubtful whether the integrative and service-oriented approach to drinking problems will continue in the future. One of the main reasons why preventive concerns were not given much weight in the transformation of alcohol control policies was that drinking problems were, in a way, absorbed by the expanding treatment system. If this assertion is correct, then we may also expect alcohol problems to become more of a social as well as moral issue in the future.

A moral issue?

The crisis in the treatment system as a mechanism for handling drinking problems seems to have brought about a revival of public concern about drinking. The growing interest in healthy lifestyles generally may also contribute to an increasing acceptance that alcohol is not simply a commodity to be enjoyed but something that entails social and health risks, as do other unhealthy items in the diet.

The possible revival of drinking as a moral issue may reinforce tendencies towards the punitive and disciplinary control of individual deviant drinkers. At the same time, it is possible that preventive control policies may regain popular support. In mass moral sentiments, these two options are not necessarily alternatives to each other. Nevertheless, from a policy perspective the distinction between individualized repressive control and preventive alcohol control policies may become increasingly salient. The singling out of individuals for special handling, whether in the form of treatment or punishment, often carries with it adverse side-effects, such as their permanent identification as deviants. Preventive alcohol policies should therefore be given high priority as an alternative to the morally inspired control of individual problem drinkers.

The approaches adopted by social and health workers in the community may have an important impact on future policies. If their frustration about the contribution of drinking to their daily caseload and the limited opportunities for coping with the problems through treatment is channelled into support of preventive policies rather than sheer despair, public health interests may indeed counterbalance economic alcohol interests more effectively. The experience of the community response project seems to warrant a certain amount of optimism about mobilizing health personnel for preventive action.

Economic factors

To the extent that the vision of slower-growing or even declining alcohol consumption is correct, the industry is likely to experience serious problems of adjustment and over-capacity. The wine surplus is likely to grow in the future. The investments made in the 1970s in the production of beer and spirits will not wear off until towards the end of the 1980s. Protection policies may call forth further investments despite the contracting world consumption of beer and spirits. International competition will intensify as producers seek compensation for contracting domestic markets. It is particularly likely that producers in the industrialized parts of the world will intensify their investment and marketing efforts in developing countries in an attempt to win new customers.

There has been a duality in the state's action on alcohol. On the one hand, preventive considerations have carried little weight in the formation of economic policies affecting alcoholic drinks. On the other, the social and health agencies responsible for the handling of alcohol problems have taken little interest in the economics of alcohol. There is an urgent need to combine these two approaches in alcohol policy decisions. In some cases, a reorganization of responsibilities among branches of government may be required to achieve a successful combination of economic, social and health considerations.

In the context of international trade agreements, alcohol is often treated like any other commodity. The export of alcohol or of alcohol production capacity brings economic benefit to the exporting country, with none of the costs associated with domestic consumption. To bring to bear, at the international level, consideration of the health and social costs associated with the alcohol trade may require mechanisms for the expression of international control interests, perhaps similar to those that already exist for the opiates and for harmful additives to food. As an interim step, international organizations should pay close attention to existing and future trade policies and arrangements that have the potential to affect the availability of alcoholic drinks.

References

1. **Rootman, I. & Moser, J.** *Guidelines for investigating alcohol problems and developing appropriate responses.* Geneva, World Health Organization, 1984 (WHO Offset Publication No. 81).
2. **Mäkelä, K. et al.** *Alcohol, society, and the state. Vol. 1: a comparative study of alcohol control.* Toronto, Addiction Research Foundation, 1981.
3. **Single, E. et al., ed.** *Alcohol, society and the state. Vol. 2: the social history of control policy in seven countries.* Toronto, Addiction Research Foundation, 1981.

The implications for other countries of the final report on phase I of the WHO project on community response to alcohol-related problems

Although the overall picture of alcohol problems may vary from place to place, there are many similar features and the experience in the three countries studied suggests that a number of the elements that should be incorporated into an improved response will be common to many communities and nations. The following seem to be among the most important.

A coordinating mechanism for collating and monitoring information on the range and extent of alcohol problems and current responses to them should be established to obtain new information and to develop relevant policies and programmes. At both the community and the national level, such a mechanism would imply the involvement of people and bodies with a variety of skills, interests and levels of influence.

Preventive measures should be developed that are likely to include both controls on the availability of alcoholic drinks and education aimed at reducing demand for them.

Measures aimed at minimizing the harmful consequences of alcohol consumption should be developed. They could include attempts to reduce the health and social consequences not only for the individual drinker, but also for the drinker's family, fellow-workers and the broader community.

Further community action research projects should be developed along the lines of the present WHO project. Every such project should, however, be adapted to suit local purposes and requirements.

Finally, there are some indications from the findings of this project that international trade in alcoholic drinks may have implications for national and local policies and programmes. Further international investigation is required into the increasing commercial production and distribution of alcoholic drinks and the consequences for the population groups affected.

3

Production of and international trade in alcoholic drinks: possible public health implications

B.M. Walsh

This chapter summarizes the main developments in the production and international distribution of alcoholic drinks over the last 25 years. It does not claim to be comprehensive because of the disparate nature of the subject and the absence of a systematic survey of the available material. The aim is a modest one, namely to summarize the main trends and features of the market in alcoholic drinks and to examine the relevance of these developments for public health issues.

World Production of Alcoholic Drinks

There is no readily available figure for the global production of alcoholic drinks. Since 1965, the United Nations *Yearbook of industrial statistics (1)* has produced tables for the production of beer, wine and distilled alcoholic drinks (spirits) by country. Table 1 summarizes the information on world alcohol production available from this source. It is the most comprehensive summary available of world production trends, although it is possible to obtain partial information on individual drinks for some earlier years. A major deficiency of these data is, however, that they do not provide information on spirits production in the USSR, which is unfortunate in view of the high reported level of consumption of vodka and other distilled drinks in that country. Since it is also impossible to obtain reliable estimates of the production of traditional fruit- or cereal-based alcoholic drinks in Africa, Asia and Latin America, this survey is limited to the more commercialized drinks and unavoidably neglects the role of a whole range of non-traded drinks about which we know very little.

It can be seen that the world production of alcoholic drinks grew from 823.9 million hl in 1965 to 1295.2 million hl in 1980. In both years beer constituted by far the largest component of the total, rising to over two thirds of total production in 1980. This comparison involves adding together litres of beer, wine and spirits, which differ greatly in alcoholic strength, so that the resultant totals may not be very meaningful. For this reason Table 1 also includes data on the world production of alcoholic

Table 1. Estimated world production of alcoholic drinks, 1965 and 1980

	Original quantities				100% alcohol[a]			
	million hl		%		million hl		%	
	1965	1980	1965	1980	1965	1980	1965	1980
Beer	503.9	892.4	61.2	68.9	22.7	40.1	33.7	39.3
Wine	287.2	341.3	34.9	26.4	31.6	37.5	46.9	36.7
Spirits[b]	32.6	61.4	4.0	4.7	13.1	24.5	19.4	24.0
Total	823.9	1295.2	100.0	100.0	67.3	102.3	100.0	100.0

[a] To convert the original quantities to pure alcohol it was assumed that beer, wine and spirits contained 4.5%, 11.0% and 40.0% alcohol by volume, respectively.

[b] Excluding the USSR.

Source: *Yearbook of industrial statistics (1).*

drinks in terms of their content of pure alcohol. In 1965, production totalled 67.3 million hl of alcohol, and by 1980 this had risen to 102.3 million hl, an increase of 52% over the period. This represents an annual average rate of increase of 2.8%. Although impressive, this growth is actually less than that recorded in industrial production or real GNP over the same period.

The data in Table 1 reveal that wine has been losing its share of the world alcohol market. Whereas in 1965 almost half (46.9%) of all alcohol production was in the form of wine, by 1980 this had fallen to below 37%. The share of spirits had risen by almost a quarter, from 19.4% to 24%, and that of beer by 17% (from 33.7% to 39.3% of the total). By 1980, beer had replaced wine as the most important source of alcohol consumption in the world, while spirits are the fastest growing drink in this market. Moreover, if spirits production in the USSR were to be included in these figures, the share of spirits in the total would rise significantly. An estimate of the consumption of spirits in the USSR (2) may be used to estimate that spirits production was in the region of 22 million hl (or 8.8. million hl of pure alcohol) in 1980. Inclusion of this in Table 1 would raise spirits' share of the world market in alcohol to 30%, and reduce the share of wine and beer to 34% and 36%, respectively.

International Trade in Alcoholic Drinks

During the 1950s and 1960s international trade grew at a very rapid pace. This reflected the high growth rates of real national income attained in the world's main trading nations together with the stable currency and liberal trading environment that were established after the Second World War and maintained throughout these decades. With the collapse of the system of stable exchange rates during the years 1971–1973, and the disruption of world economic growth in the aftermath of the rise in oil prices in 1973 and then in 1978/1979, world trade has grown less rapidly in recent years.

The growth of international trade over the postwar years gave rise to a substantial increase in the importance of international trade income relative to national income in all countries. Even in a large and relatively self-sufficient nation such as the United States, the share of imports and exports in GNP approximately doubled (from 4% to 8%) between 1960 and 1980. In the smaller European countries, dependence on international trade reached very high levels during the 1970s. In Belgium, Ireland, Luxembourg and the Netherlands for example, imports and exports were equal to, or greater than, 50% of GNP towards the end of the 1970s.

This growth of world trade has had a major impact on the range of goods and services available for consumption. There has been a progressive reduction in the distinctiveness of the consumption patterns of national populations, and a growing pervasiveness of a lifestyle based on similar consumer products and brands. While this tendency has undoubtedly enlarged the range of alternatives open to the citizens of individual countries and contributed in no small measure to the improvement of their living standards, its implications for the more traditional, small-scale firms catering to local markets have been less benign.

The difficulties posed for these enterprises by vigorous international competition have in recent years led to frequent calls for abandoning the liberal trade principles that formed the basis of the postwar expansion, but these sectional appeals have not so far resulted in a significant retreat to protectionism.

It is against these general developments in international trade that the trends in trade in alcoholic drinks should be reviewed. In Table 2, estimates of the total value of international trade in alcoholic drinks among the world's market economies are shown for 1976 and 1980. The 1980 total of just over US $9000 million represents only about 0.5% of world trade in all commodities. In 1980, the share of wine in the total trade in alcoholic drinks was 45%, spirits' share was 43% and beer accounted for only 12%.

Table 2. Estimated value of international trade in alcoholic drinks, 1976 and 1980 (market economies only)[a]

	1976		1980	
	US $ million (current prices)	%	US $ million (current prices)	%
Beer	572	12.7	1047	11.5
Wine	1886	41.8	4108	45.2
Spirits	2051	45.5	3926	43.2
Total	4509	100.0	9081	100.0

[a] Based on export data.

Source: *Yearbook of international trade statistics (3).*

In general, alcoholic drinks do not constitute an important component of international trade. Table 3 summarizes their relative importance for those countries in which they are a significant component of total trade. Only in France, Portugal and Spain do exports of alcoholic drinks in 1980 reach or exceed 2% of the value of all exports. In previous years Belgium, Ireland and the United Kingdom would have been included in this list, but the importance of exports of beer from these countries has recently declined markedly. Indeed, it is also true that in France, Portugal and Spain, where the exported wine (and to a lesser extent spirits) constitutes a relatively large share of total exports, this share has declined significantly since 1973. It is striking that even in the case of Portugal, where exports of alcoholic drinks are of greater relative importance than in any other country, total wine

Table 3. International trade in alcoholic drinks as a proportion of trade in all commodities, in selected countries, 1962, 1973 and 1980

	Imports of alcoholic drinks as a percentage of all imports (by value)			Exports of alcoholic drinks as a percentage of all exports (by value)		
	1962	1973	1980	1962	1973	1980
Belgium	0.8	0.8	0.8	n.a.	2.1	0.2
Canada	0.1	0.1	0.5	1.4	0.9	0.6
Czechoslovakia	n.a.	0.5	0.3	n.a.	0.4	0.6
France	3.9	0.9	0.5	3.2	3.5	2.6
Germany, Federal Republic of	0.7	0.8	0.6	0.2	0.3	0.3
Ireland	1.0	0.9	0.5	4.2	1.6	1.3
Italy	n.a.	0.5	0.3	1.2	1.7	1.3
Netherlands	0.1	0.5	0.5	n.a.	0.7	0.5
Portugal	n.a.	0.4	0.1	7.6	7.2	5.3
Spain	n.a.	0.4	0.2	4.6	4.2	2.2
United Kingdom	1.0	1.4	0.8	n.a.	2.4	1.8
United States	2.0	1.4	1.0	n.a.	0.6	0.1
Yugoslavia	0.1	0.1	n.a.	1.2	0.9	0.8

Source: *Yearbook of international trade statistics (3).*

production has been stagnant since 1961, while new industrial sectors have been growing rapidly and contributing to exports.

The importance of alcoholic drinks in imports is even smaller than in exports. There is no country apart from the United States for which imports of alcoholic drinks constituted as much as 1% of all imports (by value) in 1980. Imports to the United States, which is by far the largest market for imported alcoholic drinks, amounted to almost US $2500 million in 1980 or just 1% of all American imports.

The smaller relative importance of imports to exports of alcoholic drinks illustrates an important feature of international trade in general. Economic theory leads us to expect that a relatively small number of countries are likely to specialize in a commodity, such as wine, that requires special conditions, not found in many areas of the world, for its successful production. International trade allows countries whose natural resources do not favour the production of this drink to obtain it at a lower price than would otherwise prevail. The pattern of specialization that has emerged for wine and spirits is typical of that found for many other products (especially those with a basis in agricultural crops).

Of course figures on the relative importance of alcoholic drinks in total trade can mask the fact that, for specific regions within countries, dependence on the income obtained from a particular alcoholic drink may be very high. Switzerland is an example of a country where alcoholic drinks are insignificant relative to GNP or total trade, but where in certain regions the income of small farmers is supplemented to an important degree by revenue from the sale of wine and distilled products. This gives these products greater prominence in the political economy of the country than would be suspected from the aggregate statistics.

Beer

Production
World production of beer has grown spectacularly over the postwar years. Between 1960 and 1979 output expanded from 403.5 million hl to 889.0 million hl. This represents an average growth rate of 4.25% annually during a period when world industrial production grew at an annual average rate of about 5.5%.

The growth rate of beer production has not, however, been uniform over this period (see Fig. 1). Between 1960 and 1973, beer production grew at a fairly steady rate, averaging 4.8% annually. Between 1973 and 1979, growth in production slowed to an average of 3.1% annually. Although this mirrors the slowing down of industrial production generally since 1973, beer production has in fact held up well relative to most other sectors.

The distribution of beer production among the regions of the world is very uneven. In some of the world's most populous countries, beer production is insignificant, while some of the small European countries have long-established brewing industries. The growth of production has also been very uneven. In Table 4 the world's beer producers are grouped according to their output in 1960. In that year there were ten countries with production in excess of 10 million hl, which collectively accounted for over 75% of world beer production. By 1979, these ten countries had increased their production by almost 200 million hl (thereby accounting for over one third of the growth in world production) but their share in total output had fallen to 60%.

Above-average growth rates in beer production were achieved in the large group of countries whose production was between about 1 million hl and 10 million hl in 1960. Many of the 22 countries in this category doubled their production over the period. In some of them (e.g., Bulgaria, Japan, the Netherlands, Romania, Spain and Yugoslavia) spectacular growth rates were recorded. Most of these countries also achieved very high growth rates in industrial production and living standards.

The third group of countries shown in Table 4 are those where beer production was small or non-existent in 1960, but where it had grown to about 1 million hl or more by 1979. Some of the larger of these countries

28

Fig. 1. World beer production, 1965–1979

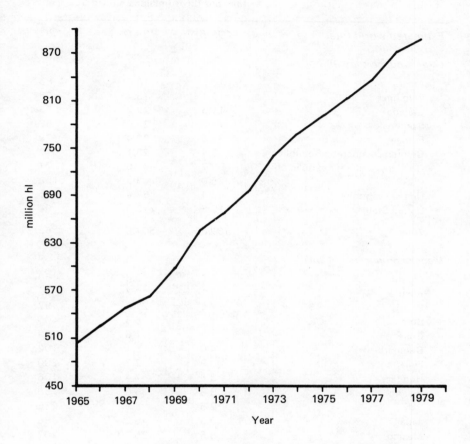

Source: *International statistical handbook (2).*

(Nigeria, the Philippines, the Republic of Korea and the United Republic of Cameroon, for example) had become major beer producers by world standards by the end of the period. While in the case of the Republic of Korea, beer production grew during a period of rapid economic development, the same cannot be said of Nigeria, the Philippines and the United Republic of Cameroon, where beer production has grown much faster than the overall volume of industrial production.

29

Table 4. Beer production by country groups, 1960 and 1979

Country	1960 (millions hl)	1979 (millions hl)	Increase (%)
Estimated world total	*403.5*	*889.0*	*120*
Large producers in 1960			
Australia	10.5	19.4	85
Belgium	10.1	13.7	36
Canada	11.5	22.2	93
Czechoslovakia	14.1	23.6	67
France	17.3	22.4	29
German Democratic Republic	13.4	23.1	72
Germany, Federal Republic of	53.7	91.6	71
USSR	25.0	63.3	153
United Kingdom	43.4	67.4	55
United States	110.8	215.3	94
Total	*309.8*	*501.0*	*63*
Medium producers in 1960			
Algeria	1.2	0.6	- 50
Austria	5.1	7.7	52
Brazil	7.5[a]	22.3	197
Bulgaria	1.1	5.5	400
Chile	1.3	1.6	23
Denmark	4.0	8.1	102
Finland	0.9	2.7	200
Hungary	3.6	7.4	106
Ireland	3.8	6.0	58
Italy	2.5	8.9	256
Japan	9.3	45.2	386
Mexico	8.5	25.7	202
Netherlands	3.6	15.4	328
New Zealand	2.5	3.8	52
Peru	1.5	4.6	206
Poland	6.7	11.3	68
Romania	1.6	9.8	512
Spain	3.4	19.7	479
Sweden	2.4	4.0	67
Switzerland	3.3	4.1	24
Venezuela	2.4	6.4	167
Yugoslavia	1.6	11.3	606
Total	*72.3*	*232.1*	*221*

Table 4 (contd)

Country	1960 (millions hl)	1979 (millions hl)	Increase (%)
Small producers with very rapid growth			
Angola	0.1	0.8	700
Bolivia	0.2	1.1	650
China	1.2[b]	5.0	317
Cuba	0.2[a]	2.3	900
Ecuador	0.4	2.3	475
Greece	0.4	2.5	525
India	0.2[a]	1.2	500
Kenya	0.4	2.1	425
Nigeria	0.2	6.7	3250
Philippines	0.9	7.3	711
Portugal	0.4	3.6	800
Republic of Korea	0.2	6.4	3100
Thailand	0.1	1.6	1500
United Republic of Cameroon	0.2	3.0	1400
Total	*4.9*	*43.9*	*796*

[a] 1965.

[b] 1970.

Source: *International statistical handbook (2).*

Despite the dramatic growth rates exhibited by several of the countries in the third section of Table 4, their share of world beer production remains relatively minor, especially when account is taken of the total population living in these areas. The countries included in this section collectively accounted for only about 5% of world beer production in 1979, although over one third of the world's population lives in them. Production of beer had increased by about 40 million hl in 1979 compared with 1960 in this group of countries. While this is a dramatic rise from the low level of production recorded in 1960, its absolute magnitude can be put into perspective when one considers that beer production in the Federal Republic of Germany alone grew by 38 million hl over the same period.

Despite the rapid growth of beer production recorded in countries such as the Philippines and the Republic of Korea, their consumption of beer per person in 1979 had reached only about 15 litres, compared with the level of over 100 litres per person in several northern European countries. This is not to deny that the rapid growth of beer production and beer drinking in several relatively low income countries has been attended by serious social and public health problems. The view could certainly be taken that the developed countries, with their long history of high levels of alcohol consumption, are not very well placed to moralize about the possible effects of rapid increases in consumption on newly industrializing or developing countries. It is also possible that in some cases the rapid growth in the production of beer has, at least in part, represented a replacement of traditional drinks whose consumption was unrecorded. In the absence of data on these drinks, there is no reliable way of estimating the importance of this factor.

The importance of beer among alcoholic drinks can be gauged from the fact that it is now the dominant source of alcohol in a group of countries with relatively high levels of alcohol intake. The list includes Australia, Austria, Belgium, Canada, Czechoslovakia, Denmark, the German Democratic Republic, the Federal Republic of Germany, Luxembourg, New Zealand, the United Kingdom and the United States. Even though in most of these countries beer's share of the alcohol market has declined significantly in recent years, it has risen in other countries that are traditionally spirits-drinking (the Netherlands and the United States) or wine-drinking (France, Italy, Portugal and Spain). Moreover, beer appears to be the (commercially produced) alcoholic drink that is first adopted in developing countries in Latin America, Africa and Asia. The effect of these trends has been for beer to displace wine in terms of share of the world alcohol market, as has been discussed earlier (pp. 23–24).

International trade
In Table 5 the importance of international trade in beer is shown for all those countries where it is important in relation to domestic beer consumption or production. The importance of trade has been measured on the basis of exports as a percentage of domestic production and imports as a percentage of apparent consumption (which is defined as domestic production minus exports plus imports).

A number of generalizations can be based on these figures. In the first place, trade in beer is generally of little importance in relation either to domestic production or domestic consumption. Exports are over 10% of domestic production in Belgium, Czechoslovakia, Denmark, Ireland, Luxembourg and the Netherlands only. Imports account for as much as 10% of consumption in Hungary, Italy and, in recent years, France only. It is interesting to note that even in countries such as the Netherlands, where beer exports are very important relative to domestic production, they do not constitute a sizeable proportion of the value of total exports (see pp. 26–27).

There is only a handful of instances where the annual trade in beer between individual countries is as large as 1 million hl. These are:

— 2.5 million hl imported by the United States from the Netherlands

— 2.0 million hl imported by the United States from Canada

— 1.6 million hl imported by France from Belgium

Table 5. Importance of international trade in beer
in relation to domestic production and consumption
of beer, 1975 and 1981

Country	Exports as a percentage of domestic consumption		Imports as a percentage of domestic consumption	
	1975	1981	1975	1981
Australia	0.9	1.7	0.1	n.a.
Austria	2.0	4.0	4.0	3.6
Belgium	13.8	16.2	9.2	7.2
Canada	2.4	9.0	0.6	1.7
Czechoslovakia	6.9	10.4	—	—
Denmark	24.4	16.0	0.3	—
Finland	1.2	2.2	0.3	0.1
France	2.6	2.8	8.9	11.1
Germany, Federal Republic of	2.5	3.6	0.8	0.8
Hungary	n.a.	n.a.	n.a.	14.6
Ireland	34.0	29.3	0.5	1.0
Italy	0.8	0.9	9.2	11.7
Japan	0.5	0.4	0.1	0.4
Luxembourg	46.8	47.2	9.2	8.5
Netherlands	16.3	25.5	3.5	3.0
New Zealand	1.1	0.9	0.2	1.6
Norway	6.7	2.2	0.4	0.1
Poland	n.a.	3.2	n.a.	0.4
Portugal	n.a.	3.4	n.a.	—
Spain	0.1	0.3	0.5	0.6
Sweden	0.4	n.a.	8.6	5.6
Switzerland	0.8	0.5	5.0	7.7
United Kingdom	1.4	1.2	4.4	4.3
United States	0.1	0.3	1.1	2.6

Source: *International statistical handbook (2).*

— 1.5 million hl imported by the United Kingdom from Ireland

— 1.0 million hl imported by Hungary from Czechoslovakia.

With the notable exception of the Netherlands' trade with the United States, all these trade flows are between neighbouring countries and over short distances. This is not surprising in view of the bulkiness of beer and the difficulties of storing it.

The very minor role played by imports of beer in the spectacular growth of consumption in countries such as Japan, the Philippines, Portugal, the

Republic of Korea and Spain illustrates how the market for a new alcoholic drink can expand virtually without assistance from international trade. It seems that although international trade in beer may be of considerable importance in demonstrating the existence of a potential market (as, for example, with the export of European beers to Africa and Asia) local production assumes the dominant role at a relatively early stage in the growth of the market.

Another striking feature of the data in Table 5 is the importance of two-way flows of trade in beer. Belgium, Luxembourg and the Netherlands are examples of countries where both imports and exports of beer are relatively important. This is really no more than a reflection of the relatively small scale of these economies and their openness to international trade in general. In this respect France and Italy are exceptional, since imports of beer have actually played an important part in the significant increase in beer consumption during the postwar period in these two traditionally wine-producing and wine-exporting countries. Between 1960 and 1980, beer consumption rose by 4.2 million hl in France and imports by 2.4 million hl, while in Italy beer consumption rose by 6.5 million hl and imports by 1.1 million hl. Thus in France, in particular, imports accounted for a major part of the growth in beer consumption.

These two countries are the clearest examples of the importance of imports as agents of change in the pattern of consumption of alcoholic drinks. It is interesting to note, however, that in both cases as beer consumption increased wine consumption tended to fall, with the result that total alcohol consumption actually declined, despite the growth of the market for beer.

The experience of Portugal resembles that of France and Italy, in that beer consumption has displaced wine, while total alcohol intake has fallen. Unlike the French and Italian cases, however, in Portugal the growth of the beer market was met almost wholly from increased domestic production.

Figures for the value of trade in beer are shown in Table 6. Although they reveal much the same general pattern as the volume figures, they make even clearer the dominance of the larger developed countries in this trade. The United States alone accounted for over 40% of the value of world beer imports in 1980 and France for a further 12%. The share of the United States rose steeply during the 1970s while that of the United Kingdom declined. Although exports are less concentrated, the Netherlands now accounts for nearly 31% of world exports (compared with only 17% in 1971) and the Federal Republic of Germany for nearly 18%. The nine member states of the European Community in 1980 accounted for 80% of world beer exports.

It may be concluded, therefore, that while beer's popularity has increased considerably over the last two decades, especially in areas where beer consumption was modest at the start of the period, imports have not generally played an important role in this development. As far as exports of beer are concerned, while a number of countries (all of them European countries with a long-standing tradition of excellence in brewing) have major export trades in beer, only in Luxembourg do exports account for

Table 6. Value of international trade in beer, 1971 and 1980
(market economies only)

Importing country	Imports (% share)	
	1971	1980
United States	14.9	40.8
France	10.5	12.0
United Kingdom	21.6	7.9
All other countries	53.0	39.3
Total	100.0	100.0
Total value (US $ million)	n.a.	1047

Exporting country	Exports (% share)	
	1971	1980
Netherlands	17.0	30.8
Germany, Federal Republic of	19.4	17.8
Denmark	19.0	8.8
Belgium and Luxembourg	7.0	8.9
Canada	2.0	8.1
Ireland	10.5	4.0
All other countries	25.1	21.6
Total	100.0	100.0
Total value (US $ million)	n.a.	949

Source: *Yearbook of international trade statistics (3).*

more than one third of total production, and only in the Netherlands has the importance of beer exports actually increased since 1960.

Wine

Production
Wine production follows a noticeably more erratic course than is apparent for beer or spirits. Climatic conditions exercise a marked influence on the quantity and quality of production in a season. The summers of 1977 and 1978, for example, were very unfavourable for wine production in the main vine growing regions of Europe, and production fell by more than 10% of the average of adjacent years.

Although periodic fluctuations have caused major setbacks to the industry — so that, for example, the level of production in 1977 was no higher than that of 1965 — there is nonetheless a marked underlying upward trend in wine production over the period 1965–1980 (see Table 7 and Fig. 2). The underlying rate of growth is, however, much less rapid than that for beer and spirits, and the share of wine in world alcohol markets has therefore declined. This decline occurred despite the dramatic increase in wine's popularity in traditionally beer- and spirits-drinking countries, where the increase in the consumption of relatively high quality wine was not sufficient to offset the decline in consumption of low quality wines in the traditionally wine-drinking Mediterranean countries.

Table 7. Estimated wine production (million hl)

Country	1961–1965 (average)	1979	1980
Italy	62.3	84.3	79.0
France	62.4	80.3	71.5
Spain	26.3	48.2	42.4
USSR	11.3	29.4	29.4
Argentina	18.9	27.0	23.0
United States	12.4	16.0	17.3
Portugal	12.8	11.5	9.4
Romania	5.9	8.9	8.9
Yugoslavia	5.3	6.7	6.8
South Africa	3.5	6.2	6.3
Chile	4.7	5.6	5.7
Hungary	3.8	5.2	5.7
Bulgaria	4.0	4.5	4.5
Greece	3.5	4.4	4.4
Australia	1.7	3.4	4.1
Germany, Federal Republic of	4.7	7.5	4.0
Austria	1.6	2.8	2.7
Brazil	1.4	2.9	2.7
Algeria	12.6	2.7	2.6
Czechoslovakia	0.3	1.3	1.4
Morocco	2.5	1.1	1.0
Other	5.6	6.3	8.5
World total	267.5	366.2	341.3

Source: *Yearbook of industrial statistics (1).*

Fig. 2. World wine production, 1965–1980

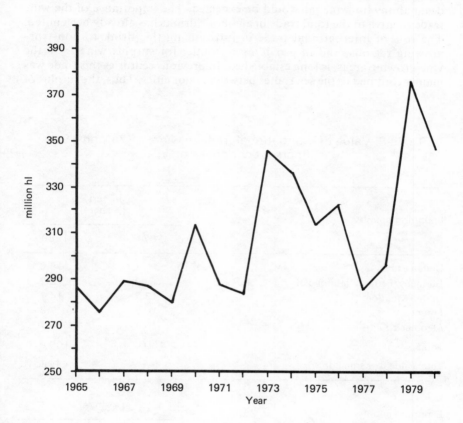

million hl

Year

Source: *Yearbook of industrial statistics (1).*

The dominance of a relatively small number of countries (France, Italy and Spain) in world wine production is evident from Table 7. In fact, these three countries accounted for 56% of world production in the early 1960s and slightly more at the end of the 1970s. Among the other wine-growing countries, production has increased rapidly in Australia, South Africa and the USSR, while two Islamic countries — Algeria and Morocco — have experienced a major decline of the industry.

International trade

In Table 8 the value of international trade in wine is shown for a number of countries. The dominance of France and Italy among exporting countries is striking and has increased since 1971. There is a wide spread of export destinations for wine, as would be expected. The importance of the wine trade relative to the total trade in alcoholic drinks has already been noted. The role of international trade in introducing this drink to non-vine-growing regions, and in providing an outlet for surplus wine from the vine-growing areas, is long established. In previous centuries this trade was mainly confined to the sea routes between major cities. Thus, the surplus of

Table 8. Value of international trade in wine, 1971 and 1980 (market economies only)

Importing country	Imports (% share)	
	1971	1980
United States	16.1	18.6
Germany, Federal Republic of	19.3	18.2
United Kingdom	13.7	14.7
France	10.8	7.8
All other countries	40.1	40.7
Total	100.0	100.0
Total value (US $ million)	n.a.	4108

Exporting country	Exports (% share)	
	1971	1980
France	40.0	44.7
Italy	20.6	21.1
Spain	9.1	9.8
Germany, Federal Republic of	4.5	8.9
Portugal	8.4	6.2
Algeria	7.1	2.1
All other countries	10.3	7.2
Total	100.0	100.0
Total value (US $ million)		3871

Source: *Yearbook of international trade statistics (3).*

wine in the inland wine-producing regions of France, for example, contrasted with the absence of such a surplus in Brittany, where a tradition of drinking low quality locally distilled drinks was established. Before the advent of the railways, the high cost of internal transport virtually precluded the expansion of an overland trade in wine. It is recounted that surplus low quality Auvergne wines were used locally to mix mortar (4).

The dominance of France as an exporter of wines should not cause us to ignore its importance as an importer. Along with the Federal Republic of Germany, it is an example of the importance of the two-way flows in the wine trade that arise when regions specialize in high quality production for export and choose to meet some of the lower end of the domestic market through imports. It is, however, at this end of the market that competition has been most intense in recent years, due in part to the decline in consumption of cheap wine in the Mediterranean region. This is reflected in the growing surplus of wine in the European Community, and in the sometimes violent protests by French producers against imports from Italy and Spain.

Spirits

Production
The information available on the world production of spirits is less complete and reliable than that on beer and wine. The principal sources used in this chapter give no information on spirits production in the USSR, which has been estimated (2) to account for about one quarter of the world production of spirits. Data for several South American countries with large distilling industries (Argentina and Brazil, for example) are not available for the 1970s. The volume of small-scale unrecorded production is probably much more important for spirits than it is for beer or wine. For all these reasons, the best that can be done is to provide a picture of the growth in production among the main producers of commercially marketed spirits.

Table 9 summarizes the available information for 1965 and 1980. Over this period world production (excluding the USSR) doubled, averaging a growth rate of 5% annually. Although this rate of growth slowed down during the recession of the mid-1970s, it accelerated again at the end of the decade.

The dominance of a few major producers is immediately evident. The growth of production in Canada, Japan, the Republic of Korea and the countries of Eastern Europe has been dramatic, and it is worth noting that in several of these countries beer production has also expanded rapidly during the same period. In some of the long-established distilling countries, such as France, the Federal Republic of Germany and the United Kingdom, growth has been much less impressive. The share of these three countries in world production fell from 30% in 1965 to 17% in 1980.

International trade
In Table 10 the value of international trade in spirits between countries with market economies is shown. Exports of spirits are dominated by Canada,

Table 9. Production of spirits by country,
1965 and 1980 (thousand hl)

Country	1965	1980
United States	7 747	14 931
Japan	2 986	6 420
Republic of Korea	893	5 051
United Kingdom	3 627	4 850
Poland	1 670	4 242
Germany, Federal Republic of	3 410	3 882
Spain	2 031	3 000
France	2 619	2 830
German Democratic Republic	775	2 095
Canada	356	1 720
Mexico	613	1 465
Czechoslovakia	369	1 259
Hungary	243	1 089
Bulgaria	411	536
Other	4 929	8 048
World total[a]	32 679	61 418

[a] Excluding USSR.

Source: *Yearbook of industrial statistics (1).*

France, the United Kingdom and the United States, which together accounted for 88% of world trade in 1971 and 84% in 1980. Trade in whisky alone accounted for over half of world trade in spirits, while brandy probably accounted for at least an additional quarter. Relatively little trade takes place between market economies in white spirits, such as gin and vodka, although these drinks may be more important in trade between socialist economies.

Imported spirits are a significant proportion of total spirits consumption in Japan, the Federal Republic of Germany, the United Kingdom and the United States only. In these countries imports of whisky and brandy constitute an important supplement to domestic sources of supply. In the United States about one third of apparent consumption is of imported spirits. The corresponding figure for the United Kingdom is about one fifth.

For countries that have specialized in high quality spirits production, exports are of considerable importance relative to domestic production. Over four fifths of the United Kingdom production of spirits is exported, amounting to somewhat less than 2% of total exports from that country. Less than half of French spirits production is exported, while a smaller

Table 10. Value of international trade in spirits,
1971, 1979 and 1980 (market economies only)

Importing country	Imports (% share)		
	1971	1979	1980
United States	47.8	31.6	n.a.
Germany, Federal Republic of	7.4	8.3	n.a.
United Kingdom	5.1	7.3	n.a.
Japan	1.8	7.0	n.a.
All other countries	37.9	45.8	n.a.
Total	100.0	100.0	100.0
Total value (US $ million)	n.a.	3456	3926

Exporting country	Exports (% share)	
	1971	1980
United Kingdom	50.4	49.6
France	20.3	25.7
Canada	15.4	6.8
United States	2.1	1.8
All other countries	11.8	16.1
Total	100.0	100.0
Total value (US $ million)	n.a.	3911

Source: *Yearbook of international trade statistics (3).*

percentage of Canadian output is sold abroad, mainly to the United States. Exports of Irish spirits (whiskey, in particular) amount to about half the total production and are sold mainly in the United Kingdom and the United States.

Attempts to develop markets (mainly in the United States) for imported white spirits have met with limited success, because of the difficulty of maintaining a distinctive market for drinks that can be readily imitated by local distillers.

General Trends in Production and International Trade

The aim of this chapter has been to draw together available data on the production and distribution of alcoholic drinks. Because of difficulties in

41

obtaining comparable information on the global production of spirits and because of the absence of information on traditional fermented and distilled drinks in less developed countries, this task has been difficult to complete satisfactorily. The main features are, however, clear enough.

The production of beer and spirits grew rapidly over the period 1960–1980. Beer experienced especially rapid growth and is now probably the most important source of alcohol consumption in the world. Wine consumption has grown less rapidly than either beer or spirits, although international trade in wine has expanded significantly.

The dominance of the large, wealthy countries of Europe and North America in the production of alcoholic drinks, and in international trade in them, has survived the rapid growth of beer and spirits production in some less developed countries. High levels of domestic production, consumption and trade in alcoholic drinks are still closely associated with high living standards and with established traditions of brewing, distilling and wine-making.

A tendency for traditionally wine-consuming societies to switch to beer has been noted, but in most cases this owed relatively little to international trade and was due mainly to the growth of a domestic brewing industry. In some of the areas where beer production has grown most rapidly, such as Japan and the Republic of Korea, spirits production has also grown spectacularly.

Many of the features of the growth of production and trade in alcoholic drinks that have been outlined in this chapter reflect the operation of forces similar to those that have governed the production and distribution of manufactured goods in general during a period of rapid economic growth. These include the effects of rationalization and technical change in reducing production and transportation costs. Little that has been uncovered in this chapter appears to be specific to the alcoholic drinks industries. Any public health implications of the rapid growth in consumption of the products of these industries therefore derive from the nature of the products themselves rather than from any special features of the industries that produce them.

Implications for Public Health

Economists are far from unanimous in their views about the implications for human welfare of the trends in the production and distribution of alcoholic drinks. There is a liberal, non-interventionist tradition that would argue that the introduction of a new commodity, or a significant reduction in the price of an existing one, can only make consumers better off by increasing the range of alternative consumption patterns available to them. If the consumers respond by increasing their consumption of the commodity in question, they reveal a preference for the new consumption pattern over the older one, which is still available. According to this view, we must respect the consumers' ability to judge what is best for their own welfare.

In line with this philosophy, we could regard the increasing popularity of beer in France and Italy as the release of purchasing power that in the past was spent on low quality wine owing to the restricted range of choice open to consumers at that time. The growth of beer drinking in less developed countries may similarly be regarded as a welcome extension of the narrow range of drinks that had been available in these countries in previous years. Beer in particular may be regarded as a relatively cheap source of some vitamins and carbohydrates, and on these grounds a welcome addition to the restricted diet of people in less developed countries.

These liberal views on the merits of the growth in the consumption of alcoholic drinks may be reinforced by considering the advantages of brewing, for example, as a productive sector in a developing country. With its relatively simple technology and use of agricultural inputs, brewing could be regarded as a suitable sector for encouragement in the earlier phases of industrialization. The lessons learned and the profits earned in this sector could play a seminal role in fostering other industrial sectors. Finally, the growth of beer consumption may also provide a convenient object of taxation in countries where the direct tax base is extremely narrow.

For all these reasons, some economists argue *(5)* that the growth of consumption of alcoholic drinks in less developed countries should be welcomed as a sign of improving living standards and nascent industrialization.

Needless to say, this sanguine view of the diffusion of the popularity of alcoholic drinks is not shared by all economists. Several of the assumptions implicit in the foregoing arguments may be queried. On the question of the benefits of increased consumption, it is obvious (even to economists) that alcohol is not simply another commodity to be analysed in the same terms as shoes or radios. One way in which it differs from most commodities is the importance of past levels of consumption for the choices and decisions made by the consumer today. The implications of this habit-forming or addictive aspect of alcohol have been studied by economists *(6)*. A lack of foresight or awareness on the part of the neophyte consumer of the longer-term implications of his current decisions undermines many of the traditional conclusions of economic theory regarding the benefits of consumer sovereignty.

Similarly, the fact that drinking has "external" or "spill-over" effects on the welfare of people other than the drinker also conflicts with the assumptions used to justify the liberal economic view. The social benefits derived from drinking are fewer than the private benefits by the amount of these external factors, yet only the perceived private benefits are taken into account in individual consumer decision-making. The social costs of drinking are well documented and include violence, accidents, illness and premature death. Many of these lead to claims for increased public spending, so that even the additional tax revenue obtained from increased consumption is not a net gain to the treasury. Increases in the rate of taxation of alcoholic drinks may be justified by reference to these considerations *(7)*.

Even the nutritional benefits of beer have been questioned in a study of the effects of drink on working-class living standards in Victorian Britain, which concluded that alternative foods such as bread consistently represented better value in the household budget *(8)*.

It would be misguided to try to evaluate in a global manner the relative merits of these conflicting views of the growth of drinking. The weight that should be attached to its advantages and disadvantages varies from country to country. In terms of practical implications, it seems obvious that neither view should be endorsed to the exclusion of the valid elements in the other. Attempts to prevent the introduction of alcoholic drinks in non-Islamic developing countries are unlikely to be very effective, but governments in these countries should be alerted to some of the inevitable adverse repercussions of the growth of drinking and be prepared to try to cope with the resultant increase in alcohol-related problems. The challenge for public health specialists in countries with long experience in this area lies in formulating specific recommendations that will guide less experienced policy-makers in learning to deal with their new problems.

References

1. *Yearbook of industrial statistics.* New York, United Nations, 1965–1980, Vol. II.
2. *International statistical handbook,* 2nd ed. London, Brewers' Society, 1981.
3. *Yearbook of international trade statistics.* New York, United Nations, 1965–1980, Vol. II.
4. **Weber, E.** *Peasants into Frenchmen: the modernization of rural France, 1870–1914.* London, Chatto & Windus, 1977, p. 216.
5. **McLure, C.E. & Thirsk, W.** The inequity of taxing iniquity. A plea for reduced sumptuary taxes in developing countries. *Economic development and cultural change,* **26**: 487–503 (1978).
6. **Houthakker, H.S. & Taylor, L.D.** *Consumer demand in the United States, 1929–70. Analysis and projections,* 2nd ed. Cambridge, MA, Harvard University Press, 1970.
7. **Walsh, B.M.** The economics of alcohol taxation. *In:* Grant, M. et al., ed. *Economics and alcohol.* London, Croom Helm, 1983.
8. **Dingle, A.E.** Drink and working-class living standards in Britain, 1870–1914. *Economic history review,* **25**: 608–622 (1972),

4

Public health aspects of the marketing of alcoholic drinks

M.J. van Iwaarden

At the time of the Depression the British drink trade had already been concerned for some years with the "capture of the younger generation growing up", as the *Brewers' journal* expressed it. These tactics did not meet with approval from the Royal Commission on Licensing of 1929–1939, which commented *(1)* as follows:

> We are unable to accept the contention that the effect of liquor advertising is merely to transfer demand from unadvertised to advertised beverages. That admittedly is one of the results, but all advertising experience establishes that the advertisement of goods of any particular brand tends to swell the total demand for all goods of that kind.

In a nutshell this is what the present discussion of the public health aspects of alcoholic drink advertising is still about. There are two aspects to the discussion — namely, the supposed harmful influence on the younger generation and the theory of shifting market shares versus the aggregate demand hypothesis.

There are, however, further resemblances between the prewar period and the present. For instance, the Royal Commission on Licensing "could think of no way of limitation which would not be open to substantial objection" *(1)*. It seems that in most countries the drink industry has never lacked defenders in parliament. While British schoolchildren in the 1930s were wearing lapel badges in praise of stout, nowadays sports sponsorship, free gifts, shirts with brand names on them and other subtle kinds of alcohol promotion look very much the same.

Public health concern with the marketing of alcoholic drinks relates to the following topics.

— Do advertising and the presentation of alcohol in other ways in the media influence our drinking habits and especially those of the younger generation in an undesirable way?

— What is the scope for restricting alcohol advertising without inducing too many adverse repercussions?

The second question in particular will be examined in relation to marketing practice and to the scope for legislative restrictions within the broader context of public opinion with respect to alcohol control policy measures.

Alcohol Advertising and Public Health

Advertising and alcohol consumption

Advertising as such is inherently linked with the economic system of free enterprise. The policy question is to what degree advertising should be allowed to promote patterns of consumption that are generally thought to be socially undesirable. Alcohol advertising that can be seen as promoting consumption patterns potentially harmful to public health, is therefore a phenomenon in which state intervention may be legitimate. This is especially likely to be the case within the broader context of an alcohol control policy.

The argument of the alcohol industry has always been that advertisements merely shift market shares and do not raise the total consumption of alcoholic drinks. They are supported in this by a number of extensive studies into the effects of advertising (2–5).

On the other hand, there are also several well documented research projects that point out that a total demand effect should not be precluded (6–8). In view of the complexity of the research field and the substantial commercial implications of policy recommendations, it is not difficult to foresee that this controversy is likely to last for some considerable time.

Most of what can be asserted about the relationship between alcohol advertising and alcohol consumption can be summarized as follows.

— Advertising is a necessary though not a sufficient condition for a successful sales campaign (market shares) (9).

— The existence and especially the direction of a causal link between the total amount of alcohol advertising and *per capita* consumption remains not proven (total demand) (2).

— Insofar as a relationship exists, it is a reciprocal one (9) (see Table 1 for Dutch figures on alcohol consumption per drinker, and mass media advertising expenditure during the period 1968–1982).

— Consumers scarcely react to a rise in the aggregate advertising budget, while the drink trade reacts very elastically to a shift in *per capita* alcohol consumption (9).

To focus on this last point, it may be fruitful to widen the scope of the present international discussion about alcohol advertising, without delving too deeply into the previous three issues. We shall thus be concentrating on social policy questions that relate to commercial publicity. Before that, however, an appraisal of advertising from the producers' point of view will be made.

Table 1. Alcohol consumption per drinker[a] and mass media advertising expenditure on alcoholic drinks in the Netherlands, 1968-1982

Year	Mean consumption per drinker (litres of pure alcohol equivalent)	Total press/radio/television advertising expenditure in million Dfl (constant 1968 guilders)	Radio/television advertising expenditure as a percentage of all press/radio/television advertising expenditure	Alcoholic drinks advertising expenditure as a percentage of all press/radio/television advertising expenditure
1968	7.42	12.6	22.0	4.8
1969	8.30	11.0	26.3	4.2
1970	9.05	11.0	27.1	4.2
1971	9.62	13.2	29.7	5.1
1972	10.45	16.0	35.5	6.4
1973	11.66	18.5	34.5	4.9
1974	12.36	18.5	37.9	5.1
1975	12.78[b]	17.9	38.5	4.9
1976	12.85	17.9	38.0	4.7
1977	13.13	20.3	35.1	4.7
1978	13.27	21.3	36.4	4.5
1979	13.17[b]	22.0	33.9	4.4
1980	13.01	20.6	29.0	4.2
1981	13.00[b]	19.3	28.3	3.8
1982	13.05	22.2	30.3	4.3

[a] Estimated percentage of the total adult population who are drinkers: 1968-1970 — 84%
1971-1974 — 85%
1975-1978 — 86%
1979-1982 — 87%

[b] Corrected for stock purchases anticipating the tax increases on spirits on 1 January 1976 and 1980, and on beer on 1 January 1982.

Source: Produktschap voor Gedistilleerde Dranken (10); Bureau voor Budgettencontrole (11); de Zwart, W. (12).

The producers' point of view

An important function of advertising is to inform consumers about the existence and features of a new product or about any improvements made to a current product. Advertisements for alcoholic drinks in general do not fulfil this function. Really new drinks are now seldom developed and little can be done to improve a can of beer or a bottle of whisky, given the price/quantity relationship. Even the introduction of a new brand of beer or spirit is rare, at least in the Netherlands.

For the alcohol producer, advertising has several different functions. Advertising is a more or less necessary condition of the whole marketing approach, simply because all competitors advertise. The risk of erosion of a carefully nurtured market share is all too real for an individual firm *(13)*. In the second place, alcohol advertising functions as a barrier to manufacturers who might want to enter the market. Because of the large sums spent on advertising by current producers, a potential entrant would have to be prepared to invest a very substantial amount of money into launching a new drink. In most cases the entrepreneur will lack such a large budget or will not be willing to take the financial risk. Together with the tendency towards concentration that characterized the 1970s, this might be a reason for the present oligopolistic nature of the supply side of the alcohol market. It should, however, be mentioned that economic theory is divided with respect to the hypothesis that advertising creates an entry barrier.

Third, alcohol advertising in general tends to confirm and strengthen people in their current behaviour rather than shaping new patterns of consumption. Alcohol advertising portrays current drinking behaviour in combination with certain attractive lifestyles that appear normal or within reach of normal aspirations. The social acceptability of alcohol advertising may be especially important for particular drinks and brands. Beer brands are presented as thirst quenchers and as inducing fun; spirits are portrayed as stimulating appetite and as relaxants; while wine is promoted as the sophisticated concomitant of a good dinner. At least in the Netherlands, this is currently the way in which alcoholic drinks are commercially presented. Now, if a particular firm succeeds in associating one brand with particular, desirable, lifestyles then this brand achieves some kind of status in specific consumer groups. Brand advertising in such a situation only has to uphold and strengthen that symbolic function to attract new buyers.

In this respect, mention has been made in several countries of advertising campaigns that are aimed at specific consumer groups whose consumption is on the increase *(14)*. The youth market in particular would seem to be approached by associating the use of specific brands with commonly accepted aspirations such as success in life, sexual attractiveness, sportsmanship, fun and so on. In this respect it should be noted, however, that a study that analysed the content of several thousand alcohol advertisements in magazines and on television did not support these assertions as far as the United States is concerned *(15,16)*. Only 3% of the magazine advertisements associated alcohol with affluence and only 7% contained explicit sexual connotations. Furthermore, the content analysis suggested that heavy alcohol consumption was not, in general, encouraged in the advertisements. Alcohol advertisements were shown to be less common in magazines for women and youth than in magazines aimed at those interested in science and the arts.

In the fourth place, advertising very often serves as a support for marketing campaigns in the distributive sector. Retailers are supplied with displays for a certain brand, discount pricing is temporarily introduced and sometimes free gifts or lotteries are combined with the consumer's purchase of that specific brand. All this is then reinforced by radio and television

48

commercials and advertisements in the press. A saturation mass media campaign is set up for a certain period. Thus, the retailers are prone to give that brand temporary prominence in their shops. A recent survey *(17)* of the Dutch retail trade in alcoholic drinks pointed out that "... radio and TV advertising by producers does have a significant effect on the purchasing behaviour of the clients". The question is whether this is a substitution or a total demand effect.

Last but not least, the tax deduction of expenditure on advertising should be mentioned. Strictly speaking, this is not a "function" of alcohol advertising, but the fact that such expenditure is regarded as an investment in future sales and goodwill makes it deductible from corporate profits before tax. This must make a lot of difference to the total volume of expenditure on commercial publicity by the alcohol industry. Since, for instance, in the Netherlands the tax on corporate profits amounts to 48%, it can be argued that the state subsidizes half of such expenditure.

The presentation of alcohol

Quite apart from advertising itself, there are other examples of the presentation of alcohol in everyday life that may influence drinking habits. The liberalization of alcoholic drinks control laws, the disappearance of puritan drinking norms and the subsequent enormous rise of alcohol consumption in most countries since the 1950s have given rise to another kind of public presentation of alcohol and drinking. The increase in portrayals of drinking on prime-time television may do no more than mirror increasing consumption trends in the general population. As noted by the British Central Policy Review Staff *(14)*, however, "those in the media who portray alcohol on television are themselves likely to be a heavy drinking group, possibly unaware that their standards are not those of the population at large".

Generally, there could be at least three ways of trying to reduce the number of drinking occasions on television. First, an attempt could be made to persuade opinion leaders in the electronic media that showing a lot of drinking on television is undesirable from a public health point of view, especially when drinking is portrayed as an appropriate mechanism for coping with stress. A second approach might be to strive at a kind of code, similar to that which has reduced the number of cigarettes smoked in American television serials, although it needs to be recognized that drinking is a functional part of the story in some films. A third approach could be to aim a small alcohol information campaign at those working in the media. This happened in the Netherlands several years ago, since it had been shown that they were at high risk of alcohol problems.

The Scope for Restrictions

Public opinion

It has not yet been clearly demonstrated that restrictive measures on alcohol advertising have a significantly moderating effect on the overall level of alcohol consumption. Equally, there is no evidence that a ban on television commercials, for example, will lead to the prevention of certain undesirable drinking patterns. Although legislative restrictions on alcohol cannot be scientifically justified, it may be that, from a sociopolitical viewpoint, government initiatives in this field can be seen as rational. Especially if an alcohol control policy is to be developed, then it is important for the government to express its concern and do something about prevailing alcohol use and its concomitant abuse.

There are few countries in which this political decision has been made. In some of the Scandinavian countries there is a virtually complete ban on alcohol advertising, the origins of which can be traced back to the social history of alcohol control policies. In Belgium, New Zealand and Switzerland a ban on television commercials has been introduced, while in Canada radio and television advertising of spirits is forbidden. The effectiveness of these measures has not been thoroughly studied. In 1976 in British Columbia, however, no significant effects on the monthly or yearly *per capita* alcohol consumption were found as a result of a 14 months' ban on radio and television advertising *(18)*.

The fruitfulness of isolated measures against alcohol advertising should be questioned. In the Netherlands, the conclusion has been drawn that restrictions on alcohol advertising should not be implemented in isolation *(19)*, although this by no means excludes the political desirability of such restrictions as one element in a comprehensive alcohol control policy. Public opinion may indeed make this a necessary condition, since raising taxes on alcoholic drinks, limiting the number of on- and off-premise outlets and setting up an alcohol information campaign may be unacceptable to the population and lacking in credibility unless restrictions on advertising are implemented at the same time.

The Dutch alcoholic drinks industry is itself currently developing a more restrictive version of the code of behaviour regarding advertising. In addition, some producers include messages about moderation in their advertising or advise consumers to refrain from drinking if they intend to drive. It may therefore be useful to ask ourselves why the alcohol industry always seems to be strongly in favour of alcohol information campaigns[a] when the constituents of alcohol control policies are being discussed. Of course, they too dislike alcohol abuse since it is disadvantageous to their case in the public debate. It may, however, also be because these campaigns are supposed to have only a negligible effect on total consumption, thus enabling the alcohol industry to use information campaigns as an alibi. Be this as it may, the point is that, in general, a larger segment of public opinion will be in favour of alcohol information campaigns than would, for example,

---

[a] In the Netherlands during the 1950s, the Central Bureau for Distilled Beverages consistently promoted the moderate use of alcohol. *Per capita* alcohol consumption in those days was only a quarter of the present level. At present, the Arbeitskreis Alkohol in the Federal Republic of Germany and the Distilled Spirits Council of the United States are proposing alcohol information campaigns. It can certainly be argued that their main reason may be to prevent stricter control measures being introduced.

50

support the introduction of higher alcohol prices. The MORI survey in the United Kingdom made this obvious (20). The question to be asked is whether the most effective measures are socially the least acceptable and vice versa?

What kind of legislative restrictions?

If it is agreed that an alcohol control policy should include legislative restrictions on alcohol advertising, the question still remains as to the precise nature of such measures. Three separate aspects can be distinguished: effectiveness, public support and adverse consequences. The first of these has been shown to be of minor importance, since methodologically it is almost impossible to isolate the supposed effect on consumption of restrictive measures on alcohol advertising.

Public support is vital. Just as relatively few people actively oppose alcohol information campaigns, so there will be relatively little resistance to proposals to place restrictions on advertising. A recent survey in the Netherlands (21) showed that only one out of five people was against the prohibition of alcohol advertising, half the public was in favour and 26% had no strong opinion.

The third aspect — adverse consequences because of alternative sales tactics by the alcohol industry — should in my opinion be taken seriously since brewers, distillers and wine manufacturers have at their disposal several other marketing strategies designed to increase sales (9).

Greater price competition by way of discount pricing at the retail level might result from an advertising ban, as might intensified promotion campaigns in the retail trade. The overall effect of these measures could well be to enlarge total demand. Furthermore, in the case of a ban on radio and television commercials, insidious advertising on television, through mechanisms such as sports sponsorship, might well intensify. The portrayal of alcohol consumption in regular television programmes will, of course, also continue.

Yet another argument for being cautious about introducing harsh control measures against alcohol advertising is shown by the figures in Table 2.

Table 2. Production value[a] and advertising expenditure on tobacco products and alcoholic drinks in the Netherlands, 1982

	Production value (million Dfl)	Expenditure on press, radio and television advertising (million Dfl)	Expenditure on advertising as a percentage of production value
Tobacco	1100	38	3.5
All alcoholic drinks	5500	48.5	0.9

[a] Production value = total consumer spending on tobacco/alcohol minus excise duties and value added tax.

In the Netherlands there has never been any television advertising of tobacco products because of the self-imposed code of the tobacco industry. Thus, in 1978, tobacco advertisements were officially banned from radio and television. As Table 2 shows, however, tobacco is marketed four times more heavily than alcohol. Of course, one might argue that this is because the industry is counteracting the anti-smoking campaigns and the growth of anti-smoking public sentiments. Since this argument seems too simplistic to account entirely for the difference in intensity between alcohol and tobacco advertising, it might be argued that the absence of tobacco commercials from radio and television in the Netherlands is an important contributory factor. If so, it would be interesting to compare the Dutch situation with figures from other countries.

Again, because of worldwide marketing strategies, a national ban on alcohol advertising will be resisted by producers on the grounds that their current market shares might fall.[a] The overall picture of exactly what would happen in the case of a ban on alcohol advertising is, however, rather vague. There are many possible lines along which industry and government might go.

The possible alternative of some kind of a settled agreement seems, therefore, quite appealing at first sight, especially if it could lead to a very strict code of behaviour for advertising and could include propaganda supporting moderate alcohol use. This is not appropriate, however, within the terms of a rational alcohol control policy. It would be difficult to convey to the public that such controls as higher alcohol taxes and stricter laws with respect to on- and off-premise outlets are necessary, while not simultaneously introducing a ban on alcohol advertising.

Do any other alternatives remain? A *total* ban on *all* alcohol advertising is not realistic. It does not comply with the principles of the prevailing mixed economies in the western world, and in most countries it probably could not be enacted or sufficiently enforced. Above all, a total ban would almost certainly have adverse consequences, such as more severe price competition. A more tactical approach may therefore be preferable. Politics has repeatedly been defined as the art of the possible.

Because of the higher marginal impact of television advertising and the supposed sensitivity of youth to electronic media influences, a ban on radio and television commercials for alcoholic drinks would seem to be one of the most rational alternatives. Such a step is recommended as part of an alcohol control policy.

Let us consider the consequences of this kind of limited ban. From a public health point of view, what is apparently the most penetrating form of advertising would be eliminated. On the basis of economic theory, the total amount spent on advertising would decline somewhat. There would, of course, be a large shift to alternative means of commercial publicity, such as through the press. In view of the deplorable socioeconomic situation of the

---

[a] **Walsh, B.** *Alcohol consumption, alcohol abuse and the scope for control policies in the Irish context.* Dublin, The Economic and Social Research Institute, 1979 (unpublished report).

press in most countries, this might even be regarded as "positive". Finally, national bans on radio and television advertising are necessary first steps to prevent the imminent global spread of satellite television commercials for alcoholic drinks. Much international cooperation and coordination will still be necessary, of course, to achieve longer-term goals.

Should a ban on radio and television commercials be considered sufficient restriction on advertising in the broader context of developing an alcohol control policy? The answer must be no; there are too many alternative ways to spend large sums on alcohol promotion. The current practice of deducting all expenditure on alcohol promotion should therefore also be questioned. It would be very interesting to see what would happen to the total volume of advertising if, for example, only half this expenditure was deductible for corporation tax purposes.

Conclusion

It has been suggested in this chapter that government decisions about the type and scope of legislative restrictions on alcohol advertising cannot be taken exclusively on rational scientific grounds, because evidence concerning the precise effects of alcohol advertising is lacking. Sociopolitical considerations must therefore play the predominant role. It has also been argued that measures to restrict alcohol advertising should not be introduced in isolation, lest these be seen to provide an easy answer to the current high levels of alcohol use and the prevalence of alcohol-related problems, while the enormous cost of alcohol abuse would in reality be ignored. Sound political choices are best guaranteed if restrictions on alcohol advertising are developed within a wider range of alcohol control measures.

The degree to which alcohol control measures are socially acceptable remains, therefore, a very important matter. Most alcohol researchers and others working in this field hold rather pessimistic views about public opinion. In the Netherlands this seems unwarranted, as is demonstrated by the results of a recent survey (21). Two thirds of the population think that preventive measures are necessary. Asked about the kind of alcohol control measures they had in mind, raising alcohol prices was most often mentioned. Furthermore, only one out of five people would be against stricter drinking age limitations or a ban on alcohol advertising, while one tenth would oppose restrictions on drinking in public places. Limiting the number of on- and off-premise outlets, however, would be met with considerable protests and negative public opinion. At least in the Netherlands, therefore, it looks as if developing an alcohol control policy is feasible.

At first sight, it seems remarkable that in many countries the alcoholic drinks industry has introduced, is currently developing or is at least prepared to think about implementing a code of behaviour for alcohol advertising. This should not, however, lead us away from the objective of changing the overall presentation of alcohol in society. The motive of the drink trade for introducing self-imposed limitations is not a concern for public health but for their own public image, and the desire to forestall stricter control measures in the distribution sector.

Banning radio and television commercials is likely to be the most promising approach, not because of its effects on consumption and abuse, but from a sociopolitical viewpoint. The sponsorship of satellite television programmes by the world's largest alcohol producers and the direction of their television commercials at large segments of the world population seem all too realistic and imminent. Only policy initiatives to ban radio and television advertising can stem this tide, and such initiatives will be impossible without sustained international cooperation and coordination.

References

1. **Turner, E.S.** *The shocking history of advertising.* New York, Ballantine Books, 1953.
2. **Bourgeois, J.C. & Barnes, J.G.** Does advertising increase alcohol consumption? *Journal of advertising research,* **19**: 19–29 (1979).
3. **Lambin, J.J.** *Advertising, competition and market conduct in oligopoly over time; an econometric investigation in western European countries.* Amsterdam, North-Holland, 1976.
4. **Schmalensee, R.** *The economics of advertising.* Amsterdam, North-Holland, 1972.
5. **Strickland, D.E.** Advertising exposure, alcohol consumption and misuse of alcohol. *In:* Grant, M. et al., ed. *Economics and alcohol.* London, Croom Helm, 1983.
6. **Leefland, P.S.H. & Reuijl, J.C.** *Advertising and industry sales: an empirical study of the German cigarette industry I/II.* Groningen University, Economics Faculty, Institute for Economic Research, 1980.
7. **McGuinness, T.** The demand for beer, spirits and wine in the UK, 1956–79. *In:* Grant, M. et al., ed. *Economics and alcohol.* London, Croom Helm, 1983.
8. *Reclame en het verbruik van Alcoholhoudende Dranken* [Advertising and consumption of alcoholic beverages]. Rotterdam, Netherlands Economics Institute, 1966.
9. **van Iwaarden, M.J.** Advertising, alcohol consumption and policy alternatives. *In:* Grant, M. et al., ed. *Economics and alcohol.* London, Croom Helm, 1983.
10. *Hoeveel alcoholhoudende dranken worden er in de wereld gedronken?* [How much alcohol is drunk in the world?]. Schiedam, Produktschap voor Gedistilleerde Dranken, 1982.
11. *Overzicht reclamebestedingen merkartikelen endiensten (1968–1982)* [Review of advertising expenditure on proprietary brands (1968–1982)]. Amsterdam, Bureau voor Budgettencontrole, 1968–1982.
12. **de Zwart, W.** *Het alcoholgebruik en het alcohol probleem* [Alcohol use and the alcohol problem]. Amsterdam, Stichting voor Wetenschappelijk Onderzoek van Alcohol- en Druggebruik, 1981.
13. **Ackoff, R.L. & Emshoff, J.R.** Advertising research at Anheuser-Bush Inc. (1963–1968), I and (1968–1974), II. *Sloan management review,* **16**(2): 1–15 and **16**(3): 1–15 (1975).

14. **Central Policy Review Staff.** *Alcohol policies in the United Kingdom.* Stockholm, Sociologiska Institutionen, 1982.
15. **Strickland, D.E. et al.** A content analysis of beverage alcohol advertising. I: Magazine advertising. *Journal of studies on alcohol,* **43**: 655–682 (1982).
16. **Strickland, D.E. & Finn, T.A.** A content analysis of beverage alcohol advertising. II: Television advertising. *Journal of studies on alcohol,* **43**: 964–989 (1982).
17. *De Structuur van het slijtersbedrijf en de commerciële mogelijkheden in de toekomst* [The structure of the retail trade and the commercial prospects]. The Hague, Economisch Instituut voor het Midden- en Klein-bedrijf, 1982.
18. **Smart, R.G. & Cutler, R.E.** The alcohol advertising ban in British Columbia; problems and effects on beverage consumption. *British journal of addiction,* **71**: 13–21 (1976).
19. **Engelsman, E.L.** *Het Nederlandse alcohol-overheidsbeleid* [An alcohol control policy in the Netherlands]. Leidschendam, Department of Public Health and Environmental Protection, 1981.
20. **Smith, R.** The politics of alcohol. *British medical journal,* **284**: 1392–1395 (1982).
21. **Garretsen, H.F.L.** *Probleem drinken* [Problem drinking]. Rotterdam, GG & GD, afdeling GVO, 1982 (Report No. 41).

5

Using health promotion to reduce alcohol problems

I. Rootman

Over the past decade, increasing emphasis has been given to the so-called control perspective by professionals working in the alcohol field in Europe and North America. The interest in, and growing acceptance of this was in large measure stimulated by the publication in 1975 of *Alcohol control policies in public health perspective (1)*. It was then heightened by the release of *Alcohol, society, and the state (2,3)* and *Alcohol and public policy: beyond the shadow of prohibition (4)* in 1981.

During this same period, there has been an increasing emphasis on health promotion by governments, health professionals and the public. This interest in and acceptance of a health promotion perspective was stimulated by the publication in 1974 of *A new perspective on the health of Canadians (5)* and was heightened by the release of *Healthy people (6)* by the United States Surgeon General five years later. The acceptance of this by governments and health professionals is shown by the establishment of a number of units with health promotion in their titles in Europe and North America, both inside and outside government. The interest of the public is demonstrated by an explosion of books on health, by an increase of media programming on health and by increasing participation in fitness activities. Finally, studies in North America and Europe have presented evidence of increased concern about preventive health by the public as well as high demand for information about health *(7,8)*.

Although these two perspectives have gained strength during the same period, and although health promotion approaches have been increasingly applied to dealing with alcohol consumption and problems, there is little evidence of collaboration between advocates of the two perspectives. One reason why this may have been the case up to now is that advocates of the control perspective are sceptical about the use of health promotion for modifying alcohol consumption and reducing problems.

This chapter will therefore begin by considering the question of what is health promotion. It will then review the evidence of the efficacy of health promotion in relation to alcohol consumption and other behaviour. It will then consider some of the incompletely explored possibilities for controlling alcohol consumption through health promotion and suggest what might be done at national and international levels to realize these possibilities. It will conclude with the suggestion that health promotion approaches in the alcohol field should not be dismissed too early and that they be seen as complementary to approaches based on the control perspective.

What is Health Promotion?

Unfortunately, as a recent review of health promotion activities in Europe and North America, carried out by the health education unit of the WHO Regional Office for Europe, amply demonstrates, there is no consensus between or within countries regarding the concept and meaning of health promotion: "Discussions which sought specifically to capture the meaning of 'health promotion' were more remarkable for the diversity of views and meanings generated than for any consistency in the use of the concept".[a] It could be argued that such diversity is to be expected and, in any case, as suggested by Simpson & Isaak (9) "variations among definitions [of health promotion] are essentially matters of preference, and cannot be characterized as right or wrong". They further suggest that "definitions are determined by the orientation of the group or agency that is generating the definition, and reflect preferences among competing theories as well as its attention to the political considerations which impinge upon it". Instead of striving for a universally accepted definition of health promotion, it might be preferable, as Simpson & Isaak suggest, to make explicit the principal options that could be taken into account in arriving at definitions suitable for particular purposes. The key step in so doing is to identify the fundamental issues that must be resolved in selecting a definition of health promotion.

The first of these issues has to do with the goals of health promotion. That is, should health promotion include the prevention of disease or various health problems, or should it be limited to the enhancement of existing levels of health? In practice many, if not most, workers in the field consider the two goals and associated benefits inseparable and the concepts of disease prevention and health promotion are often used synonymously. On the other hand, some insist that the term "health promotion" should be limited to activities designed to improve or enhance health. There is general agreement, however, that the concept of health promotion excludes illness management and rehabilitation activities.

A second important issue has to do with the appropriate target population for health promotion. That is, should health promotion activities be directed towards healthy populations, or those considered to be at risk of particular diseases or problems? No doubt, those who see health promotion as including disease prevention would be inclined towards including at-risk populations, while those who see it as health enhancement would not

---

[a] **Anderson, R.** *Health promotion: an overview* (unpublished WHO document HED/HPR 1, 1983).

necessarily exclude such populations from their definitions of health promotion. It is likely that most would exclude populations that are already suffering disease or difficulty.

A third issue has to do with the focus of the interventions. That is, should health promotion activities simply seek to change the individual or should they include attempts to change the environment as well? The review by the WHO Regional Office suggested that there was in fact general support for including both the environment and the individual, but at least some people and groups would opt to exclude the environment from their definitions.

Another, perhaps related, view has to do with whether or not health promotion activities should be limited to those of external agencies or whether they should include the efforts of individuals to promote their own health. While there was some difference of opinion on this matter, it was suggested in the WHO review that "there would be some difficulty in excluding those forms of behaviour that individuals engage in, which are of a social, political or group nature, aimed at changing the environment or living conditions".

The final important issue has to do with the types of intervention that might be included as part of health promotion. That is, should they be limited to "health education and related organizational, political and economic intervention" as suggested by a widely cited American definition (10), or should cultural, genetic, social or other interventions be included as well? It could be argued that if health promotion is seen to be individual and informal, as well as organized and external, all forms of intervention to improve health should be included.

If one accepts that these five issues need to be resolved for health promotion to be defined, then there are about 50 possible definitions that could be chosen by people, depending on their particular purposes. For the purposes of this chapter, it seems reasonable to accept the most encompassing definition possible. In other words, health promotion encompasses interventions that:

— aim at the enhancement of health as well as the prevention of disease or problems;

— involve individuals themselves as well as external agents; and

— include all types of measures designed to improve health or prevent disease or problems.

Taking such a broad definition then, what evidence is there that health promotion efforts have been effective in modifying the consumption of alcohol and associated problems or in affecting other kinds of behaviour and problems? The next section deals with this question.

The Effect of Health Promotion on Alcohol Consumption

Primary prevention demonstration projects funded by the US National Institute on Alcohol Abuse and Alcoholism during the years 1974–1978 were critically reviewed by a team of researchers in 1979 (11). All these projects involved attempts to impart or investigate knowledge, attitudes, beliefs and values about alcohol and its effects in order to promote responsible drinking. Of the 16 projects on which some information could be obtained, only 7 could be evaluated by the team. All these projects used education or training as their intervention approach. None of them used experimental designs to evaluate their outcomes: quasi-experimental designs were used by five, and non-experimental by two.

The team concluded that while results of a few projects were promising, none of them "clearly demonstrated a link between knowledge or attitude change and subsequent drinking behaviour". On the positive side, however, they concluded that "people are receptive to prevention activities, that attitudes and knowledge about alcohol are subject to change and that prevention efforts often complement treatment services and strengthen the total effort to reduce the problems of alcohol misuse and alcoholism".

Blane & Hewitt (12) carried out an extensive review of public education programmes on alcohol that used mass communication. They reviewed programmes carried out by several government agencies, as well as voluntary and commercial groups operating at both national and regional levels. Although they found many methodological shortcomings in the evaluation designs used, they concluded that "mass media messages affect attitudes and knowledge levels, but seldom make a significant impact on behaviour". They did, however, cite some examples of campaigns where there appeared to be impacts on behaviour.

One of these was a 1973 Christmas drinking/driving campaign operated collaboratively by the Addiction Research Foundation of Ontario and the Ontario Ministry of Transportation and Communication (13). This campaign emphasized citizen involvement in dealing with drinking/driving and the use of alternative means of transport. It was carried out in nine experimental communities that were compared to nine matched control communities. Radio was the principal medium of communication used, although there were other community activities in some of the towns. Among the positive effects found in the pre- and post-programme random telephone surveys, was a significant increase in the number of people in the experimental towns who reported not driving after drinking too much. There was also a greater reported number of conversations about drinking and driving.

Another campaign, that used a combination of media and other approaches and seemed to have some impact on consumption, was carried out in 1982 by the Health Promotion Directorate of Health and Welfare Canada in collaboration with the Alcoholism Foundation of Manitoba. This project took place in four northern Manitoba communities, in two of which a national media campaign was supplemented by an intensive community involvement effort. Independent samples of 200 residents in these towns were surveyed by telephone both before and after the campaign. The evaluation found that the self-reported frequency of heavy drinking was markedly lower in the experimental towns after the campaign. The researchers suggested, however, that "while this does not necessarily mean that the actual frequency of drinking declined in those towns, it would seem to indicate that there was a greater concern about heavy drinking following the campaign" *(14)*. It should also be noted that only short-term follow-up was carried out.

An innovative European campaign that also appears to have had some impact on consumption was carried out in Norway in 1981 *(15)*. The unique part of the campaign was that all Norwegians were asked to stop drinking alcohol after 11.00 p.m. on Saturday 14 November and to switch to soft drinks instead. The request was communicated through a variety of mass media techniques. Seventy per cent of a sample of the population, interviewed three weeks after 14 November, reported that they had not consumed alcohol on that date, an unusually high figure for a Saturday night in Norway. On the other hand, 11% did continue drinking after 11.00 p.m. In addition, there were no differences in the alcohol-related police calls for that day in comparison to other Saturdays in the month or in the previous year. Although there was a decline in the level of alcohol consumption in 1981, the report suggested that this was probably due to rising prices and a tighter budget. It was suggested, however, that the campaign at least provided people with an argument for drinking less.

Vuylsteek *(16)* reviewed about 50 European health education programmes for school-aged children and their parents on smoking, alcohol and non-medical drug use. Twelve of these programmes were selected to be used as background for a working group on education programmes for school-aged children and their parents. Only five dealt explicitly with alcohol, but unfortunately the results of the evaluations of these programmes were not available at the time the review was published. A report evaluating one of these programmes, the Scottish Health Education Group's campaign on alcoholism, was however subsequently published *(17)*. This mass media campaign was designed to persuade alcoholics to seek treatment, and to educate the public about alcoholism and about agencies available to help problem drinkers. It was evaluated by surveys in four communities, by monitoring referrals to alcohol treatment agencies and by analysis of letters sent in response to the campaign. Although the surveys found that the campaign did not lead to reduced alcohol consumption during the eight-month evaluation period, there did appear to be an increase in new referrals to treatment agencies immediately after the campaign, as well as an influx of letters requesting help and advice. Thus, it appeared that the campaign did have some impact on behaviour, which may have subsequently affected the consumption of high-risk drinkers.

The Addiction Research Foundation of Ontario reviewed information/ education strategies in the context of their task force on alcohol, public education and social policy which published its report in 1981 *(18)*. They considered both mass media programmes and programmes carried out in formal educational settings. With regard to the mass media programmes, the task force concluded that:

> The impact of the mass media in health-oriented alcohol education appears to be a limited effect on awareness and public attitudes. No lasting, substantial behavioural impact has been demonstrated. However, very few programs have been adequately conceptionalized or evaluated. Many programs have been

either too short in duration, not intensive enough, or lacking sufficient focus to affect substantial proportions of their target audiences with the message.

As for alcohol education in formal settings, the task force concluded that:

It is clear that alcohol education in formal educational settings can increase knowledge levels. What is not clear, however, is the relationship between increased knowledge and attitude, belief, and behaviour change with respect to alcohol. Findings in this area are mixed and somewhat sparse, but there is at present no solid evidence to indicate that school alcohol education reliably influences drinking behaviour. It must be kept in mind, however, that much of the evidence necessary for a confident conclusion regarding impact does not exist at present.

The United States National Academy of Sciences panel on alternative policies affecting the prevention of alcohol abuse and alcoholism also reviewed the effectiveness of educational strategies *(4)*. The commissioned paper on this topic reached the conclusion that:

Although it may be true that previous education campaigns focused on various aspects of alcohol abuse have had minimal, if any effect ... their apparent failures were due, not to the lack of viability of the approach, but to insufficient attention to some of the principles of mass persuasion and social learning theory that have been applied with some degree of success in related areas.

On the basis of their review of education, information and training programmes, the panel reached the following three conclusions:

— it is important to define the behaviour that is the target of the educational effort as concretely as possible;

— the emphasis should be on teaching specific new knowledge, acquiring new skills and practising techniques for maintaining the new skills;

— the programs that have been successful have adopted an experimental approach and have drawn heavily on the professional knowledge and skills of people trained in behavioural and communication sciences.

The panel also noted that educational and legal approaches were complementary, especially in relation to efforts to reduce drunken driving. They also noted the importance of symbolic action by governments in shaping drinking practices.

To sum up, the evidence for the effectiveness of health promotion approaches in controlling alcohol consumption and reducing problems is equivocal. While there are some studies that suggest that health promotion approaches can affect consumption of alcohol, most of the studies reported in the literature do not seem to support this conclusion. It should be noted, however, that the studies reviewed are not necessarily representative of all studies that have been conducted on this question, nor do they cover all possible kinds of health promotion intervention. In fact, they tend to focus on a fairly narrow range of health promotion intervention, namely mass media campaigns and educational programmes in formal settings, particularly in schools. Thus, it is possible that a well executed evaluation of other kinds of health promotion efforts may produce different kinds of conclusion. For this reason the next section will consider evaluations of health promotion interventions that do not focus specifically on alcohol.

The Effect of Health Promotion on Other Behaviour

Selected examples of health promotion intervention that appears to have been successful in changing behaviour and resulting problems will be presented.

Smoking

One such example for the field of smoking is a project carried out by McAlister and his colleagues in California (19–21). Seventh grade students were trained by peer leaders (high school students) to resist social pressures to use tobacco. After almost three years, students who received the training were smoking significantly less than a control group, as well as other ninth grade students in the same school. In addition, although the project was not aimed specifically at drinking or drug taking, it was found that frequent marijuana and alcohol use were also less prevalent among students who received training. Thus, it appears that the effective use of peer pressures may have promise as a preventive technique in relation to smoking and to other kinds of health behaviour, including drinking.

Another example from the smoking field comes from studies carried out by Warner (22,23). Using a regression model, he assessed the effects of anti-smoking advertisements on television and radio in the United States during the period 1968–1970 and found that they were associated with a significant reduction in cigarette consumption. He further suggested that this anti-cigarette publicity probably affected consumption by contributing to the support of tax increases on cigarettes. In a later study using the same techniques, he suggested that the subsequent continuing decline in per capita cigarette consumption was due to the effectiveness of the non-smokers rights movement. In other words, he concluded that the overall decline in smoking over the period he studied was due to the cumulative effect of persistent publicity supported by other public policies.

A final example from the smoking field is a British study of the effect of general practitioners' advice against smoking (24). The authors found that, after a one-year follow-up, 5.15% of those who had received advice, been given a leaflet to help them and been told that they would be followed up, were still not smoking. This compared to 0.3% of non-intervention controls, 1.6% of questionnaire-only controls and 3.3% of advice-only controls. While 5% seems like a small proportion, they point out that because of the large numbers of people seen by general practitioners, such a rate nationally would be more useful than far higher success rates using more intensive methods in specialized clinics.

63

Nutrition

In the field of nutrition, several studies recently reviewed by Levy and his colleagues *(25)* appear to show behavioural changes. For instance, one project that used demonstrations of the effects of diet alterations on the health of live rats found that students' knowledge and diet were significantly better than controls. Another study, using token reinforcements in the school food service, found significantly less plate waste. In both these cases the results were obtained without a concurrent, formal, classroom education programme.

Recent evaluations of the nutrition education and training programme in the United States *(26)* found that both centralized (single curriculum) and decentralized (multiple curricula) state nutrition education programmes had large positive effects on children's knowledge about nutrition, but smaller and less consistent behavioural and attitudinal effects.

A committee of the American Dietetic Association recently reviewed studies of the potential benefits of nutritional counselling, particularly for ambulatory nutritional care services offered in a variety of settings, including private offices, physicians' offices, outpatient clinics, community or neighbourhood health centres, public health departments or individuals' homes *(27)*. They examined the effectiveness of nutritional counselling among pregnant women, children, adults and the elderly and generally concluded that it can change dietary practices in all these groups, although often in conjunction with other approaches (e.g. providing nutrient supplements). They also reviewed the effectiveness of a number of American Government food assistance programmes. Although the data for assessing these programmes were judged to be inadequate, studies did find positive changes in nutritional practices associated with each of the programmes examined *(28)*. In conclusion, the committee pointed out that "promotion of preventive nutritional care in the health care delivery system interrelates with the food and nutrition, social welfare, and educational systems" and that " nutrition education as a component of all pertinent systems will have a synergistic effect in promoting the nutrition and health status of all people throughout the life cycle" *(27)*.

Exercise

In the field of exercise, one promotional campaign that appears to have met with an unusal degree of success was launched in Canada in 1971 by an organization called ParticipAction. This organization is independent of government, although it receives a substantial federal government grant to support its activities. It uses a variety of marketing tools, including public service advertising, corporate sponsorship, written materials and community and regional demonstration projects. According to studies undertaken by ParticipAction, less than 5% of Canadians were regularly physically active when it was founded, compared to 37%, 11 years later. It is, of course, difficult to know to what extent such changes were directly due to its influence. A recent survey found, however, that over 70% of Canadians are familiar with its message and logos and 85% think that it is effective in the sense that it has caused Canadians to become more physically active *(29)*.

An interesting study has also been reported regarding the possible impact of a daily fitness programme on the alcohol consumption patterns of residents of a treatment programme for alcoholics *(30)*. Corroborated reports obtained during follow-ups 3 months and 18 months after participation in the fitness programme, suggested that participation improved the likelihood of remaining abstinent. The authors suggest caution in interpreting these findings, because of possible confounding factors such as the uniqueness of the particular programme studied. It does, however, suggest an approach that may be worth further study in relation to both alcoholics and non-alcoholics.

Seatbelts

There is also some encouraging evidence from the safety field regarding the effectiveness of health education programmes to promote seatbelt use. For instance, a French programme effectively used modelling to facilitate seatbelt use. Letters were sent to drivers asking them to set an example by wearing their seatbelts and putting a bumper sticker on their car announcing that they were doing so. They were also asked to recruit friends to the programme. Seatbelt use significantly increased in the experimental city and not in the control city.[a]

Direct experience with seatbelts was found in one study to be more effective than passively seeing or hearing how seatbelts would work in the event of an accident through unrealistic simulations.[b] It has also been shown that people who are specifically informed that their chances of being injured in their lifetime of driving are relatively high and that seatbelt use reduces this risk, show greater changes in self-reported seatbelt use than people exposed to standard seatbelt or control messages. The effect was found to be even stronger on those "saturated" with the message *(31)*. The use of incentives has also recently been found to increase seatbelt wearing *(32,33)*.

Two other approaches that have also been shown to be effective in promoting seatbelt use are combined enforcement/public education programmes and feedback. A recent evaluation of the former approach (called the Selective Traffic Enforcement Program) found an immediate increase in seatbelt use from 58% to 80% with a decline to 66% two years later. Seatbelt use also declined during the same period in a control community. A replication of the project in 1981 resulted in an increase in seatbelt-wearing rates in the experimental community which was sustained for three months, in comparison to a continuing drop in seatbelt-wearing rates in the control community over the same period *(34)*.

---

[a] **Labadie, M.J. et al.** *Conception et expérimentation d'une campagne d'incitation au part de la ceinture de sécurité.* Unpublished paper presented at the First International Conference on Driver Behaviour in Zurich in 1973.

[b] **McKnight, A.J. & McPherson, K.** *Four approaches to instruction in occupant restraint use.* Unpublished paper presented at the 61st Annual Meeting of the Transportation Research Board in Washington, DC, in 1981.

With regard to the feedback approach, the posting of signs at the roadside giving, for instance, the percentage of drivers wearing seatbelts the day before seemed to result in small but significant increases in seatbelt use in at least two studies *(34,35)* and a substantial reduction in speeding in others *(36,37)*.

It should also be noted that one of the most successful national media campaigns on record was mounted in the driver safety field *(38)*. A television programme called *The national drivers' test* was shown by CBS television in the United States before the Memorial Day weekend, when concern for traffic safety was greater than usual. Over 30 million people watched the programme, letters were received from almost 1.5 million people and over 35 000 enrolled in driver improvement programmes shortly after the broadcast. This suggests that adequately planned and promoted campaigns for public education may by themselves succeed in promoting certain behaviour.

Heart disease

Finally, two major projects that are often cited as models for health promotion efforts are the Stanford heart disease prevention programme and the North Karelia project. Both these projects focus on modifying the major lifestyle risk factors leading to coronary heart disease.

The Stanford project, one of the largest preventive medicine research efforts in the United States, began in 1972. During its first phase, which lasted until 1975, residents of two small California towns were exposed to a heavy barrage of information on heart disease and on methods to change harmful behaviour *(39)*. In addition, intensive individual training was given in one of the experimental communities to people who were considered to be particularly susceptible to heart disease. The control community did not receive any kind of information. The results of the first phase showed positive changes in the experimental communities in comparison to the control communities. There was a 20% reduction in the total risk index and there were very significant changes in dietary practices. Changes were greater in the community where individual instruction was added to the mass media campaign, although the mass media apparently was sufficient to induce people to reduce their consumption of some high-cholesterol foods. According to the investigators,

> one can conclude that the media alone have the power to influence the risk of coronary heart disease and some related behaviour and that when face-to-face instruction is conducted in addition to the use of the media, a broader range of behaviour is susceptible to a greater magnitude of immediate and long-lasting modification.

The second phase of the project started in 1980 and will continue until 1986. It is being carried out in five cities and includes measurement of the risk factors evaluated in the first phase, plus detection of changes in the number of heart attacks and changes in mortality and morbidity related to heart disease. It uses a stronger multi-media campaign and a stronger direct communications component carried out through the participation of community organizations and health professionals. It also includes the introduction of some changes at the institutional level (e.g. weight control classes and classes to give up smoking).

The North Karelia project is similar to the Stanford project, but differs in some respects. For instance, the original initiative for the project came from the community itself and there has been a continued emphasis on community participation. From the start, the project also involved attempts to change the environment through such means as increasing the availability of low fat foodstuffs and introducing restrictions on smoking in certain indoor areas. The North Karelia project began in 1972 with the main objectives of reducing the prevalence of smoking, the serum cholesterol concentration and raised blood pressure values among the population of North Karelia (40,41). The comprehensive programme to achieve these objectives consisted of giving information to the public through a variety of means and in a variety of settings, systematically integrating the programme into existing services and creating new services when necessary, training health personnel, making environmental changes and collecting data.

Among other things, it was found that over the period studied (1972–1977), the decrease in risk factors was generally greater in North Karelia than in the control county. The smallest net reduction, however, also occurred in the prevalence of smoking. This was because smoking also decreased appreciably in the control area, possibly as a result of antismoking education in the neighbouring county and a national increase in antismoking activities.

In 1978, a two-year school- and community-based intervention was initiated by the North Karelia investigators to prevent smoking and to influence dietary habits among 13-year-olds in North Karelia. Intensive intervention was carried out in two schools, one rural and one urban, as well as general countywide intervention. Among other things the investigators concluded that "the educational program was relatively effective in preventing smoking increase among children of the critical age. The nutritional program was more effective among girls than boys" (42). They suggested that this supported the hypothesis that comprehensive educational programmes can influence health-related behaviour in adolescence although they stressed the need for further studies to confirm their experience. Other studies carried out in North America do, in fact, provide some confirmation of this conclusion (43,44).[a]

Overall, the North Karelia investigators felt that " the comprehensive community-based approach and integration of the activities into the social and health service structure of the community were particularly important factors" in the success of the project (42). While the Stanford and North Karelia projects are not without their deficiencies (e.g. each used a single

---

[a] **Hopp, J.W.** *A health education program for parents and children who exhibit high risk factors of coronary heart disease.* Unpublished paper presented at the Annual Meeting of the American Alliance for Health, Physical Education and Recreation in Kansas City in 1978.

community as a control, which does not allow estimation of the variability of the results) they do offer encouragement to those working in the field of health promotion. In particular, they suggest the value of a comprehensive, integrated approach at the community level.

To sum up this somewhat selective review of the empirical evidence for the effectiveness of health promotion approaches as applied to behaviour other than alcohol use, the overall conclusion is that the evidence is equivocal. There is certainly sufficent evidence to suggest, however, that health promotion approaches, if appropriately developed and applied, can modify behaviour to enhance health and reduce ill effects. The review also leads to a number of other specific conclusions that may be helpful in suggesting further possibilities for controlling alcohol consumption through health promotion.

How can Alcohol Consumption be Controlled through Health Promotion?

It should be apparent that the literature that has been reviewed is somewhat limited in terms of suggesting ways of reducing alcohol problems through health promotion. This is true for a number of reasons. It does not cover all the relevant programmes and interventions, because it is generally restricted to published literature, mostly from North America. Secondly, the literature varies considerably in focus and conceptual approach and, finally, there are methodological shortcomings in many of the studies cited, which suggests the need to exercise caution in reaching firm conclusions. Nevertheless, the literature does suggest a number of possibilities for the control of alcohol consumption and reduction of alcohol problems using a health promotion perspective or approach. Given the limitations of the literature, however, it may be desirable to stand back and look at the possibilities of health promotion from a more analytical and conceptual point of view. Thus, the first part of this section will consider possibilities based on the literature and the second will consider possibilities based on a more theoretical analysis.

Literature review
Some of the possibilities suggested by the material that has been reviewed are as follows:

— realistic and creative use of mass media

— innovative school education programmes

— involvement of existing health and social services

— experimentation with innovative techniques

— influencing alcohol consumption through other behaviour

— use of community involvement strategies

— use of multi-component, integrated programmes.

68

Mass media

It is clear from the literature that single, mass media campaigns by themselves are unlikely to change health behaviour substantially. They do, however, appear to be effective in changing awareness and attitudes and, as such, can create a context within which other initiatives to change behaviour can succeed. Thus, in relation to alcohol consumption it is important that mass media interventions have realistic goals that may *not* include changing behaviour. This is particularly so, given the enormous amount of advertising of alcoholic drinks. Media efforts might therefore acknowledge and pursue goals that could include increasing awareness of the need for control efforts and targeting specific groups that can be reached through these efforts.

While the evidence does seem to suggest that, by and large, media campaigns are ineffective in changing health behaviour, there is some suggestion that certain kinds of media campaign may be successful in changing this behaviour. In particular, those that are sustained over a long period of time, focus on specific behaviour and are integrated with other approaches, seem more likely to be effective. Thus, if the objective is to change alcohol consumption patterns, it would be best to use mass media as only one of the approaches with a long timeframe in mind, and with a focus on specific behaviour that may be amenable to change.

School education programmes

The literature seems to suggest that traditional educational approaches in schools are not successful in changing health behaviour. Nevertheless, some innovative approaches such as peer counselling and experimental demonstrations seem promising. Perhaps more emphasis in the alcohol field should be given to the use of such approaches.

On the other hand, it needs to be recognized that traditional health education may have a role to play as well. In particular, it can be used to provide understanding of health and disease concepts to large segments of the population and to reinforce positive attitudes. Thus, school health education can, like the mass media, help to create a context in which other initiatives to change behaviour will be more likely to succeed, particularly if efforts in the school are linked with other community health promotion efforts.

Existing health and social services

As suggested by the British study on the potential effectiveness of physicians in smoking cessation efforts *(24)* and by the research on nutrition counsellors *(27,28)*, health professionals can have an impact on various kinds of health-related behaviour. Insufficient attention seems to be given to this possibility in the alcohol field. A great deal more could be done to involve health and social service professionals in the control of alcohol consumption using health promotion approaches.

Innovative techniques

A number of innovative techniques were identified as possibly effective in modifying health behaviour. A number of the techniques in the safety field, in particular, seem to hold promise. Specifically, increasing perceived risk, modelling, and the use of incentives and feedback seem to be effective in changing behaviour. Perhaps some of these techniques could be applied to the alcohol field, at least on an experimental basis.

Use of other behaviour

Some evidence has been presented that it may be possible to modify alcohol consumption through changing other behaviour. The study on the use of fitness in the treatment of alcoholics is a case in point *(30)*. There is also other evidence regarding the interrelationships between various kinds of health behaviour. For instance, research on adolescent drug use has found that involvement with alcohol is associated with involvement with other kinds of drug, and that the use of drugs is associated with a higher likelihood of involvement in other types of risk behaviour, such as precocious sexual activities and aggression in delinquents *(45,46)*. Others have found interrelationships between various kinds of preventive health behaviour *(47)*. These findings seem to argue for a much more significant attempt to influence drinking and associated problems through other kinds of behaviour.

Community involvement strategies

Among the most promising approaches described in the literature are community-based interventions, such as the Stanford *(39)* and the North Karelia *(40–42)* projects. They have provided convincing evidence that community-based approaches to health promotion can be effective in modifying health behaviour, especially if citizens are actively involved. Some evidence from the alcohol field also points this way *(14)*. Thus it would seem desirable to continue such efforts, at least on an experimental or pilot basis. In particular, it might be useful to deal with alcohol in the context of an overall health promotion approach through the community.

Multi-component, integrated programmes

One of the lessons that the Stanford and North Karelia projects teaches us is the potential effectiveness of multi-faceted, integrated approaches. It is quite clear that if the objective is to change behaviour, it is more likely to succeed if a variety of strategies are employed, including environmental changes. This is true not only for community-based programmes, but also for those that take place in other kinds of setting such as the workplace.[a] While it is not always possible to use multi-faceted, integrated strategies because of cost and other reasons, it is certainly an ideal for which it is worth striving in the control of alcohol consumption.

In concluding this section it would be well to refer to Warner's studies of the long-term changes in cigarette smoking that suggest that efforts to modify entrenched behaviour patterns in the population do not succeed

---

[a] **Weinstein, M.S.** *Health promotion and lifestyle change in the workplace* (unpublished WHO document HED/HPR 2, 1983).

overnight *(22,23)*. They must be seen as part of a long-term, cumulative process. This is as true with respect to alcohol use as it is for other kinds of behaviour.

The use of analysis
In designing a health promotion programme in relation to alcohol, there are at least four fundamental questions that need to be answered.

— What is it that one wishes to promote or prevent?

— To whom is the programme or initiative to be directed?

— What strategies are available for achieving the objectives of the initiative?

— How, specifically, does one go about doing it?

The answers to these questions will obviously depend on who is asking them. Thus, if one is an individual wishing to promote one's own health through changing one's alcohol consumption patterns, one would have certain goals, targets (in this case, oneself), possibilities for action and available techniques. On the other hand, a health official asked by the government to design a national programme for health promotion in relation to alcohol would probably identify different kinds of goal, target, strategy and technique. The same would hold true for the medical director of a large factory, a regional planner, a researcher at a university, or an international health official responsible for alcohol programmes.

While it might indeed be instructive to put oneself in the shoes of each of these people and consider how they might answer the four fundamental questions, space precludes us from doing so. Instead, since the purpose of this publication is to examine possibilities for future action at national and international levels, it may be best to concentrate on the roles of the national and the international health officials.

There are a number of ways in which national officials might respond to the question of what one wants to promote or prevent but, as suggested in the earlier discussion of the definition of health promotion, they would first have to decide whether they were interested only in promoting something or in preventing something as well. Since most people working in the field find the concepts of promotion and prevention inseparable, it is likely that national officials would go along with the majority on this issue and would propose both promoting and preventing something.

They might, for instance, wish to promote abstention from alcohol as an overall objective of a national health promotion programme on alcohol. In many countries, however, it is unlikely that such an objective would be politically acceptable and they might therefore be more likely to opt for controlling alcohol consumption instead. Being good planners, they will have to specify what they mean by controlling alcohol consumption. That is, do they mean lowering the average level of consumption in the population, or do they mean promoting a moderate level of consumption among all individuals in the population? If they mean the latter, what would they consider to be moderate? Alternatively, they might define controlling alcohol consumption in terms of reducing the magnitude of certain consequences of alcohol use. But then they would have to specify which consequences: deaths arising from impaired driving? Drunken behaviour? Fetal effects of alcohol?

It will probably not be easy for the national official to make all of these decisions without the help of statistics and the advice of colleagues. The second fundamental question to be answered is: at whom are these programmes or initiatives to be targeted? The answer to this question will obviously depend on the answer to the first. That is, if the goal is to reduce the overall level of consumption in the population, it might be best for the target to be the population as a whole without singling out a particular group. On the other hand, if the goal is to reduce the fetal effects of alcohol, the target might be restricted to pregnant women. Similarly, if the goal is to promote moderate consumption, then the target may be immoderate drinkers, who will then have to be defined. If there is more than one goal, there may be more than one target group.

Having selected the target groups, the official will have to confront the third fundamental question of what strategies might be pursued by a government to achieve the goals of the programme in terms of the specified target groups. There are a number of possibilities here but the four major ones are likely to be:

— control

— influence

— competence development

— environmental design.

Control strategies "refer to those government actions, such as legislation, which are taken to modify a particular substance, its availability or the demand for that substance". Influence "refers to a variety of activities ranging from the provision of information to the more structured effort which attempts to modify individuals' attitudes in a certain direction". Competence development is "intended to improve individuals' skills in order to enhance their self-esteem and to improve their ability to deal with everyday life situations". Finally, the environmental design "activities attempt to reduce the stresses within and improve individuals' relevant environments — in particular, the school, the workplace and the community" (48).

While one might argue with these definitions, the strategies certainly are identifiable and the important ones are at the disposal of governments. It should be noted, however, that they might not be equally applicable to all goals. If, for instance, the goal is to eliminate the fetal effects of alcohol, it is probable that the influence strategy or perhaps the competence development strategy would be more appropriate than a control or environmental

72

design strategy. If, on the other hand, the goal is to reduce the overall level of consumption in the population, a control strategy may be most effective, although one certainly would not want to rule out the others. Similarly, if the goal is to produce moderate consumption perhaps all the strategies would be appropriate.

In any case, the national official will eventually select the strategies that are most appropriate to achieve the goals that have been specified. "Appropriate" in this case would include considerations of cost, effectiveness, available resources and perhaps political considerations as well.

Having done that, the national official will now have to decide on the specific measures that will be used to achieve the goals. Again, there are many possibilities to choose from. If, for instance, a control strategy seems most appropriate, they will be able to select from a wide range of possibilities including:

— modifying the price of alcoholic drinks;

— changing the legal drinking age;

— modifying the frequency of on- and off-premises outlets;

— changing the hours and conditions of sale;

— modifying the types of outlet;

— introducing or strengthening legislation on impaired driving, or restrictions on advertising or legislation regarding certain inebriated customers;

— establishing municipal policies regarding licensing conditions and special events permits.

Some of these may be implemented directly by national government, whereas others can only be implemented by local government.

In the latter case, the national government has the option of using an influence strategy to convince other levels of government to make the appropriate changes. As is the case for control strategies, there are many means by which influence strategies can be carried out. These include the use of mass media, formal education programmes, publication and diffusion of materials, research, workshops and a variety of intra- and intergovernmental committees and working groups.

As for competence development, this could include the compilation and distribution of resource materials, workshops for service providers as well as the public, and development of materials for programmes in specific settings such as schools, health centres and community groups and among health care professionals.

Finally, the environmental design strategy would include such measures as modifying the roads to make them safer for drunken drivers and their potential victims, providing alternative activities for the use of leisure, improving safety conditions in the workplace, and providing adequate treatment facilities.

73

To sum up, it is obvious that the planner has many possibilities to consider in designing a national health promotion programme on alcohol consumption and problems. It should also be clear by now that he or she will find only limited guidance from published material. The literature contains very little evidence regarding the relative effectiveness or appropriate mix of the four strategies and very little evidence regarding the effectiveness of particular measures or their appropriate mix. One conclusion can, however, be drawn with certainty — that a control perspective is not incompatible with a health promotion perspective. In fact, ideally, they are integral to one another.

Turning now to the predicament of the international official, it is clear that many of the same considerations that apply to the national official also apply to him or her. Nevertheless, the political reality in which an international official works is much more complex than that in which a national official works. He or she must deal with a variety of structures and social policies. Thus, in formulating a health promotion strategy relative to alcohol, the international official is even further constrained regarding the goals, target groups, strategies and techniques that can be applied.

Nevertheless, there is a good deal that can be done at this level to enhance the abilities of governments to develop appropriate policies and programmes to control alcohol consumption. In recent years WHO, for instance, has made many significant contributions to this task. It has developed a variety of resource materials, it has provided a forum in which countries can share their experiences, it has developed pilot projects such as the community response project *(49)* that can help countries implement their programmes and strategies, and it has provided symbolic leadership to the countries of the world in relation to the reduction of alcohol-related problems.

National governments need to be encouraged to implement control and promotional strategies in relation to alcohol. International organizations can support research and continue to develop materials that will aid national governments. They can also exercise symbolic influence in this field.

Conclusions

Throughout this chapter there has been an attempt to portray health promotion in a positive light. It should be recognized, however, that health promotion can have a negative side to it as well. Health promotion efforts can be seen as an attempt to modify the behaviour of the population. They have also been criticized for "blaming the victim". While these concerns certainly are legitimate ones that deserve full and honest debate, they should not be used as excuses for disregarding promising avenues for preventing or reducing alcohol-related problems. It should be evident from this chapter that there is sufficient evidence of the efficacy of the health promotion approach in the alcohol field to justify its continued and improved use.

It should also be apparent that a health promotion perspective is not in conflict with a control perspective. They can, in fact, be complementary and should be seen as such. Through judicious application of both approaches to the control of alcohol consumption and the prevention of associated problems, we shall come closer to the goal of health for all by the year 2000.

There are a number of specific actions that could be taken at both the national and the international level to realize some of the possibilities for reducing alcohol problems.

Suggestions for national action

Clarification of the concept of health promotion
There is considerable variation in the use of the concept of health promotion within countries. While it may not be possible, or indeed necessary, to reconcile such uses, it may be helpful for people working in the field at least to make them explicit. Thus it may be worthwhile for a national government or some other body to examine systematically the use of the concept within the country and to publish and disseminate their analyses.

Descriptions of health promotion approaches
A variety of health promotion approaches are being used within countries and many of the people working in the field may be unaware of what others are doing. It thus may be useful for national governments or some other bodies to collate and analyse descriptions of existing programmes so as to make them available to others working in the field. An example of such an attempt is the inventory of prevention programmes compiled by the Canadian federal provincial working group on prevention training in the addictions field *(50)*.

Support for groups carrying out health promotion activities
Health promotion activities can be carried out by a variety of bodies — individuals, social groups, communities, regions and nations. National governments are in a position to support such initiatives through a variety of means including grants, the supply of written materials, and the support of meetings and workshops. One specific action that might be taken would be to develop a set of guidelines in relation to alcohol for community action. These might be based on the experience of the WHO community response project *(51)*.

Demonstration projects
Given the uncertain state of knowledge about the effectiveness of health promotion efforts relative to alcohol, it would seem desirable to encourage and support the development of innovative pilot or demonstration projects such as the North Karelia and Stanford projects. Such projects need not be as costly or elaborate as either of these examples and might simply involve pilot-testing certain promising approaches (e.g., peer counselling) in limited settings.

Support of evaluation
Whether projects are run on a demonstration basis or not, attempts should be made to evaluate them as far as possible. In doing so, a wide range of

evaluation methods should be used (including qualitative approaches). It would be desirable for national governments to carry out evaluations of their own health promotional efforts, as well as to support evaluations of others.

Research on critical issues

Not only are evaluations of health promotion interventions required, but it should be obvious that a variety of other research is required on critical issues pertinent to health promotion. For instance, more research is required on the nature of the relationship between alcohol use and other kinds of health-compromising and health-enhancing behaviour. To what extent do they cluster together to form discreet lifestyle patterns, and to what extent is it possible to affect alcohol consumption through changing these patterns? Similarly, it would be useful to have information on the role of the social environment and of the impact of various agents of socialization (e.g., family, church, schools and the mass media) on health-related behaviour. Studies are needed on the possibilities and strategies for changing norms and influential reference groups such as peers and on the possibilities for substituting health behaviour alternatives for health-compromising ones. These are but a few of the questions that might be investigated either directly by national governments or through their support of others, with a view to improving the effectiveness of health promotion interventions in relation to alcohol.

Dissemination of results of evaluations and other research

It is not enough simply to carry out evaluations or other kinds of study. The results should be made available to people working in the field so that the experience can be assimilated. National governments are in an ideal position to collate, analyse and disseminate such results and should be encouraged to do so.

National programmes

The measures that have been suggested so far could all be part of a national programme for controlling alcohol consumption through health promotion. In addition, there are other actions that a national government could take as part of a comprehensive, coherent programme. They could, for instance, sponsor national media campaigns to heighten awareness of the problems associated with excessive alcohol use. They could also develop training opportunities for people working in the field and disseminate materials. National governments might consider embarking on such initiatives. It might be wise to plan and carry out such initiatives in the context of an integrated, national health promotion programme.

Health promotion policies

Finally, it may be desirable for national governments to attempt to develop explicit health promotion policies in relation to alcohol consumption. Such policies should specify explicit goals and attempt to clarify the relationship between health promotion approaches and approaches based on the control

76

perspective. From a symbolic point of view, governments should make the public aware of their efforts in this regard.

These are but a few suggestions for national action. There are, of course, other actions that national governments could take to develop and implement effective health promotion efforts in relation to alcohol. In any case, it should be apparent that national efforts can be worthwhile and are worth pursuing. The same is true of international efforts.

Suggestions for international action
International organizations could usefully consider the following suggestions to assist their member states in developing health promotion activities in relation to alcohol.

Promote awareness of the possibilities
One way in which this suggestion could be realized is through commissioning specific papers on this topic, ensuring that they are discussed at relevant conferences and that they are subsequently published and disseminated. In addition, it might be useful for international organizations to document examples of both successful and unsuccessful health promotion interventions in relation to alcohol, perhaps building on or collating national attempts to do so.

Evaluation research
There are a number of steps that could be taken to support and encourage evaluations of the effectiveness of health promotion efforts. Guidelines could be developed, for instance, for the evaluation of health promotion interventions, which could be distributed to member states. Workshops and training sessions could be supported on the evaluation of health promotion, and the exchange of evaluation results facilitated through publications and other means. Finally, intercountry pilot projects could be supported that focus on the evaluation of health promotion interventions in relation to alcohol.

Research on critical health promotion issues
Some of the efforts these organizations could make to support and encourage research on the critical issues of health promotion and alcohol have been noted in the national suggestions. They could commission literature reviews, publish and disseminate their results, sponsor workshops on these issues and provide fellowship and training experiences to researchers interested in working in the field.

Training opportunities and materials
International organizations are in a position to develop training programmes for professionals in member states who are working in the field or who wish to do so. Providing opportunities for exchanging ideas and producing guidelines or other materials that can be adapted to national circumstances, are both important methods of proceeding. These and other ways would

increase the capabilities of member states to carry out health promotion programmes for reducing alcohol problems.

Symbolic leadership
Finally, as was true for national governments, it is extremely important for international organizations to exercise symbolic leadership in fields that deserve to be supported such as health promotion. Symbolic leadership can be exercised by making pronouncements in the various public forums that these organizations have at their disposal, as well as through their own activities.

These are but a few of the alternatives that WHO might consider in its efforts to assist Member States to develop health promotion activities in relation to the control of alcohol.

References

1. **Bruun, K. et al.** *Alcohol control policies in public health perspective.* Forssa, The Finnish Foundation for Alcohol Studies, 1975, Vol. 25.
2. **Mäkelä, K. et al.** *Alcohol, society, and the state. Vol. 1: a comparative study of alcohol control.* Toronto, Addiction Research Foundation, 1981.
3. **Single, E. et al., ed.** *Alcohol, society, and the state. Vol. 2: the social history of control policy in seven countries.* Toronto, Addiction Research Foundation, 1981.
4. **Moore, M.H. & Gurstein, D.R., ed.** *Alcohol and public policy: beyond the shadow of prohibition.* Washington, DC, National Academy Press, 1981.
5. **Lalonde, M.** *A new perspective on the health of Canadians.* Ottawa, Government of Canada, 1974.
6. **Office of the Assistant Secretary for Health and Surgeon General.** *Healthy people: the Surgeon General's report on health promotion and disease prevention.* Washington, DC, US Government Printing Office, 1979.
7. **Bauer, K.G.** *Health — United States. Part 2: prevention profile.* Washington, DC, US Department of Health and Human Services, 1980 (PHS 81-1232).
8. **Cartwright, A. & Anderson, R.** *General practice revisited.* London, Tavistock, 1981.
9. **Simpson, R. & Isaak, S.** *On selecting a definition of health promotion: a guide for local planning bodies.* Toronto, Addiction Research Foundation, 1982 (Substudy 1252).
10. **Green, L.W.** Public policy and methodology: national policy in the promotion of health. *In: Report of the 10th International Conference on Health Education.* London, Health Education Council, 1980.
11. **Staulcup, H. et al.** A review of federal primary alcoholism prevention projects. *Journal of studies on alcohol,* **40**: 943–968 (1979).
12. **Blane, H.T. & Hewitt, L.E.** Alcohol, public education and mass media: an overview. *Alcohol, health and research world,* **5**: 2–16 (1980).

13. **Pierce, J. et al.** Experimental evaluation of a community-based campaign against drinking and driving. *In:* Israelston, S. & Lambert, S., ed. *Alcohol, drugs and traffic safety.* Toronto, Addiction Research Foundation, 1975.

14. **CanWest Research Corporation.** *Dialogue on drinking: tracking the impact on four northern Manitoba towns.* Ottawa, Health Promotion Directorate, Health and Welfare Canada, 1982.

15. **Waahlberg, R.B.** *Report on a mass media attempt to change behaviour, 14 November 1981.* Oslo, Norwegian Directorate of Alcohol and Drug Problems, 1982.

16. **Vuylsteek, K.** *Health education: smoking, alcoholism, drugs.* Copenhagen, WHO Regional Office for Europe, 1979 (EURO Reports and Studies, No. 10).

17. **Plant, M.A. et al.** Evaluation of Scottish Health Education Group's 1976 campaign on alcoholism. *Social psychiatry,* **14**: 11–14 (1979).

18. *Public education social policy.* Toronto, Addiction Research Foundation, 1981.

19. **McAlister, A. et al.** Pilot study of smoking, alcohol and drug abuse prevention. *American journal of public health,* **70**: 719–721 (1980).

20. **McAlister, A. et al.** Adolescent smoking: onset and prevention. *Pediatrics,* **4**: 650–658 (1979).

21. **Perry, C.L. et al.** Adolescent smoking prevention: a third-year follow-up. *World smoking and health,* **5**: 40–45 (1980).

22. **Warner, K.E.** Cigarette smoking in the 1970s: the impact of the anti-smoking campaign on consumption. *Science,* **211**: 729–731 (1981).

23. **Warner, K.E.** The effects of the anti-smoking campaign on cigarette consumption. *American journal of public health,* **67**: 645–650 (1977).

24. **Russell, M.A.H. et al.** Effect of general practitioners' advice against smoking. *British medical journal,* **279**: 231–235 (1979).

25. **Levy, S.R. et al.** Nutrition-education research: an interdisciplinary evaluation and review. *Health education quarterly,* **7**: 107–126 (1979).

26. **St. Pierre, R.G. & Rezmovic, V.** An overview of the national nutrition education and training program evaluation. *Journal of nutrition education,* **14**: 61–66 (1982).

27. **Popkin, B.M. et al.** The benefits and costs of ambulatory nutritional care. *In: Costs and benefits of nutritional care, phase I.* Chicago, American Dietetic Association, 1979.

28. **Owen, A.L. et al.** Health and nutritional benefits of federal food assistance programs. *In: Costs and benefits of nutritional care, phase I.* Chicago, American Dietetic Association, 1979.

29. *Behaviour and attitude toward physical activity among Canadians.* Toronto, ParticipAction, 1982.

30. **Sinyor, D. et al.** The role of a physical fitness program in the treatment of alcoholism. *Journal of studies on alcohol,* **43**: 380–386 (1982).

31. **Schwalm, N.D. & Slovic, P.** *Development and list of a motivational approach and materials for increasing use of restraints.* US Department of Transportation, 1982 (Final Technical Report, PFTR-1100-82-3).

32. **Geller, E.S. et al.** A behavioural analysis of inactive strategies for motivating seatbelt usage. *Journal of applied behavioural analysis,* **15**: 403–415 (1982).

33. **Hunter, W.W. & Stutts, J.C.** Use of economic incentives to modify safety belt use behaviour. *In: 26th Annual Proceedings of the American Association for Automotive Medicine, Ottawa, 1982.* Morton Grove, IL, American Association for Automotive Medicine.

34. **Jonah, B.A. et al.** Promoting seatbelt use: a comparison of three approaches. *In: 26th Annual Proceedings of the American Association for Automotive Medicine, Ottawa, 1982.* Morton Grove, IL, American Association for Automotive Medicine.

35. **Nau, P. & van Houten, R.** The effects of prompts, feedback and an advertising campaign on the use of safety belts by automobile drivers. *Environmental systems,* **11**: 351–361 (1982).

36. **van Houten, R. & Nau, P.** *A study to assess the effects of feedback signs on driving speed.* Ottawa, Road Safety Branch, Transport Canada, 1982.

37. **van Houten, R. et al.** Analysis of public posting reducing speeding behaviour on an urban highway. *Journal of applied behavioural analysis,* **13**: 383–395 (1980).

38. **Bush, W.V.** *The national driver's test.* New York, Random House, 1965.

39. **Meyer, A.J. et al.** Skills training in a cardio-vascular health education campaign. *Journal of consulting and clinical psychology,* **48**: 129–142 (1980).

40. **Puska, P. et al.** *Community control of cardiovascular diseases: the North Karelia project.* Copenhagen, WHO Regional Office for Europe, 1981.

41. **Puska, P. et al.** Changes in coronary risk factors during comprehensive five-year community programme to control cardiovascular diseases (North Karelia project). *British medical journal,* **279**: 1173–1178 (1979).

42. **Puska, P. et al.** The North Karelia youth project: evaluation of two years of intervention on health behaviour and CVD risk factors among 13–15-year-old children. *Preventive medicine,* **11**: 550–570 (1982).

43. **Coates, T.J. et al.** Heart, healthy eating and exercise: introducing and maintaining changes in health behaviours. *American journal of public health,* **71**: 15–23 (1981).

44. **Podell, R.N.** Evaluation of the effectiveness of a high school course in cardiovascular nutrition. *American journal of public health,* **68**: 573–576 (1978).

45. **Jessor, R. et al.** *Psychosocial factors in adolescent alcohol and drug use: the 1978 national sample study, and the 1974–78 panel study.* Boulder, CO, Institute of Behavioural Science, 1980.

46. **Jessor, R. & Jessor, S.L.** *Problem behaviours and psychosocial development: a longitudinal study of youth.* New York, Academic Press, 1977.

47. **Langlie, J.K.** Interrelations among preventive health behaviours. A test of competing hypotheses. *Public health reports,* **94**: 215–225 (1979).

48. **Torjman, S.R.** *Conceptual framework for preventive action.* Ottawa, Health Promotion Directorate, 1983.

49. **Ritson, E.B.** *Community response to alcohol-related problems.* Geneva, World Health Organization, 1985 (Public Health Papers, No. 81).

50. **Torjman, S.R.** *Addictions prevention: selected programs.* Ottawa, Health Promotion Directorate, 1982.

51. **Rootman, I. & Moser, J.** *Guidelines for investigating alcohol problems and developing appropriate responses.* Geneva, World Health Organization, 1984 (WHO Offset Publication No. 81).

6

Four country profiles

Italy — *A. Cottino & P. Morgan*[a]

Italy, like many other nations, has a multifaceted history of attitudes, beliefs, and concerns about the problems of alcohol consumption, mixed with drinking patterns that are pervasively integrated into society. Thus, elucidating the history of alcohol control in Italy becomes a search into the political, scientific and cultural history of the country itself *(1)*.

The origins of the alcohol question
The question of the problems of alcohol surfaced during a period in the nineteenth century when at least three major historical forces combined: the influence of the international temperance movement; the growth of an Italian urban proletariat; and the development of a school of positivist criminological thought that began to reshape ideas of crime, causality and social control. Added to this was a nascent public health approach to medical science within which the problems of alcohol consumption began to be introduced.

A social problem
Thus, major discussions on the question of alcohol in Italy began at the time of the Industrial Revolution, when the new bourgeois state was suddenly faced with a whole series of problems, better known under the general heading of *la questione sociale* (the social question). The use and abuse of alcohol became inextricably bound to questions of vital importance for the existing class structure, such as the question of workers' wages (which tended to be fixed at a subsistence level because of the large reserve army), of bad nourishment and of crime. As a background to this trend, the political speeches and official statements of leading government representatives of the period are filled with explicit references to the threat to social stability

---

[a] Alcohol Research Group, University of California, Berkeley.

posed by the so-called "dangerous classes". In spite of the strong opposition of leading socialists such as Colajanni (2) and Pistolese, two related views advanced by Lombroso and his followers became dominant by the beginning of the twentieth century (3). One stated that alcohol abuse had organic causes and the other that it strongly correlated with crime. The defeat of the socialist standpoint had far-reaching consequences. It established the centrality of the alcohol question as an issue of law and order, while emphasizing the growing importance of medical responses to problems of alcohol abuse and alcoholism. In addition, it paved the way for regulating the number of alcohol outlets in relation to the size of the population.

It was those changes in the definition of the alcohol problem that shaped the discussion within the Italian temperance organizations, as well as establishing the path of alcohol control laws for subsequent decades. Meanwhile, the rise of the Italian urban proletariat altered drinking customs and contributed to an increase in overall *per capita* alcohol consumption.

An examination of *per capita* consumption trends from 1881 to 1940 reveals a dramatic increase in wine consumption in the period before the First World War (Table 1). Spirits consumption, on the other hand, seems to have peaked in the 1880s. In fact, it was the sharp increase in spirits drinking after 1860 that sparked the initial concern over alcohol problems in Italy (4). This increase can be attributed to a tendency for alcohol products to be seen increasingly as ordinary commodities (E. Forni, unpublished observations, 1983).

Table 1. Annual *per capita* consumption of alcoholic drinks
in Italy, 1881–1940

Year	Spirits (litres)	Wine (litres)	Beer (litres)	Total (litres of pure alcohol equivalent)
1881/1890	1.74	95.2	0.8	13.28
1891/1895	1.22	93.4	0.58	12.77
1896/1900	1.15	91.8	0.55	12.53
1901/1905	1.34	114.2	0.82	15.55
1906/1910	1.02	128.6	1.63	17.29
1911/1915	0.32	127.0	2.14	15.44
1916/1920	0.63	93.5	1.93	11.59
1921/1925	0.72	111.1	3.58	13.79
1926/1930	0.55	109.9	2.86	13.58
1931/1935	0.24	90.7	1.13	11.76
1936/1940	0.25	84.2	1.41	10.28

Source: 1881 to 1910 figures taken from Wlassak, 1928.
1911 to 1940 figures taken from *Annuario statistico dell' agricoltura Italiana*, 1939/1942.

The temperance movement

The first temperance organization in Italy, *La Società di Temperanza,* was formed in Turin in 1863. Other temperance organizations were started in the last decades of the nineteenth century and in the early twentieth century, principally in the provinces north of Rome. They were fundamentally middle class in orientation, although many involved the active participation of important national political figures. Unlike many of their counterparts across the Atlantic and in northern Europe, they generally did not espouse total abstinence. The Italian Temperance League founded in 1892, for example, divided its members into three categories: total abstainers; abstainers from distilled liquors; and "honorary" members *(4)*.

Like their counterparts elsewhere, however, Italian temperance groups were particularly concerned with drinking among the urban proletariat. Although a call for outright prohibition was seen as impossible in a country such as Italy, measures of control on the availability of alcohol and against the public display of drunkenness were explicitly demanded. The concern over public (working-class) displays of intoxication led the *Società di Temperanza* in 1879 to draw up a resolution calling for the suppression of drunkenness by legal means *(4)*. Ten years later, under the directorship of Zanardelli, the National Minister of Justice, who was involved in the temperance movement, the first penal code resolutions were passed against public drunkenness as "offensive or dangerous to the public". This law also punished those who "caused" such a state of intoxication in another. In 1930, this law was amended to include any manifestation of drunkenness in a public place.

Restrictions on working-class drinking taverns began in 1913 with a law limiting the number of establishments to one for every 1000 inhabitants. According to one temperance publication, however, the "enforcement of the law was very lukewarm, because the then all-powerful statesman Mr Giolitti had no intention of provoking the ire of the liquor traffic" *(4)*.

Economic interests

That statement is evidence of the economic importance of wine production in Italy during this period. Italy ranked second only to France in worldwide production of wine. Furthermore, production had increased considerably from an average of 700 million gallons (over 30 million hl) per year in the 1880s to over 1000 million gallons (just over 45 million hl) per year between 1909 and 1913 *(4)*. It was estimated that, during these years, Italy accounted for over a quarter of the world's wine production.

Economic strength was not merely limited to production interests. It was estimated that the number of on-premises consumption outlets, such as inns, taverns and cafes, increased from 146 075 in 1874 to 167 492 in 1884. In 1886 it was estimated that there was one on-premises drinking establishment for every 160 people. Consequently, it may be assumed that the producers and distributors of alcohol were a substantial political and economic force in Italy.

The Italian temperance movement reached its peak at about the same time as did consumption, which averaged over 125 litres *per capita* a year between 1906 and 1913, the year in which the Italian temperance movement played host to the Fourteenth International Congress against Alcoholism.

The First World War brought an end both to the debate and to the activities of most temperance organizations. No further alcohol control laws were passed until the rise of Fascism, when the alcohol question was reformulated in terms based on (although in many ways different from) those used in the debate in the late nineteenth century.

The Fascist period

Most of Italy's alcohol control laws date from the Fascist period. These are laws limiting availability and setting restrictions on outlets and on the production and distribution of alcoholic drinks, as well as provisions in the penal code on issues of alcohol and crime. To Mussolini, alcohol was a threat to the growth and development of the strong Italian worker, and he kept the issue of immoderation at the forefront of both health and social control agendas.

The temperance and prohibitionist groups formed during this period were all coordinated by the state-run Italian Central Committee against Alcoholism. There were attempts to lower grape production in the "battle for grain" campaign, where Mussolini urged that cereals should be substituted for wine grapes. There were also attacks on the legislative front, with laws curbing the availability of alcohol by placing limits on location and creating age restrictions.

Thus, a real revolution took place in the way legislators consider alcohol in relation to criminality. The 1931 Penal Code — also known as the Rocco Code — reversed the previous principle, according to which being drunk was an extenuating circumstance. Thus, not only was drunkenness in public places punished but, of greater significance, more severe sanctions were applied to crimes committed by drunken persons. It has also been inferred (5) that Mussolini discerned a connection between the inn and the political opposition, since thousands of inns were forced to close within the space of only a few years.

Despite these efforts, however, Mussolini admitted in 1939 that his alcohol policy had been a failure (6). Although official records show that consumption decreased by around 10 litres *per capita* per year (see Table 1) he was unable to alter the basic patterns of alcohol consumption in Italy.

The alcohol question since the Second World War

The postwar period in Italy has witnessed both change and stability on the alcohol question. The link between alcohol and crime, which had developed within the nineteenth century criminological debate and was carried through the Fascist period, has today faded from the scene almost completely. For the past 30 years, a narrow psychological view of alcohol problems has prevailed, coupled with a drug-oriented therapeutic approach closely tied to the mental health profession. In fact, with the exception of a brief flurry of research activity during Italy's "miracle" modernization period of the late 1950s and early 1960s, there has been almost no professional or public attention drawn to the non-medical consequences of

86

alcohol consumption. On the other hand, both consumption levels and drinking patterns have remained relatively stable. Italians today do not really drink very differently from the way they did 50 or 60 years ago. An analysis of consumption patterns during the last 30 years (see Table 2) reveals that Italians generally drink less wine, more beer and more spirits, but that their overall consumption has changed very little. Indeed, compared with some other European countries, the general trend has been a modest decline. Drinking patterns have remained essentially the same, although with some important changes. Wine is still the main drink of choice in Italy, and is still drunk chiefly at meals.

The old inn now competes with new institutions. Although it still exists in parts of the urban north and in the rural south, it has been replaced largely by the snack bar, which emerged as the neighbourhood meeting place with

Table 2. Annual *per capita* consumption of alcoholic drinks in Italy, 1950 to 1980

Year	Spirits (litres of pure alcohol equivalent)	Wine (litres)	Beer (litres)
1950	0.7	83.0	3.4
1952	0.7	89.7	3.1
1954	1.0	99.5	3.3
1956	0.8	107.4	3.5
1958	1.0	107.0	3.8
1960	1.0	108.3	5.1
1962	1.3	108.3	7.4
1964	1.6	103.8	8.3
1966	1.5	110.6	9.8
1968	1.6	116.0	10.7
1970	1.8	113.7	11.5
1972	1.9	110.9 (101)[a]	12.6
1974	2.1	109.2 (103)[a]	15.0
1976	1.9	98.0 (92)[a]	14.1
1978	2.1	91.0 (86)[a]	14.9
1980	1.9	93 (87)[a]	16.7

[a] The Italian Statistics Institute, from which the wine consumption figures are taken, changed its reporting procedure in the 1970s to include some non-alcoholic drinks made from grapes. The figures in parentheses are taken from EEC data on *per capita* wine consumption in *Commission Report to the Council on the foreseeable developments in the planting and replanting of vineyards in the Community and on the ratio between production and utilization in the wine sector*, 1981.

Source: Produktschap voor Gedistilleerde Draken, 1981.
Brewers Association of Canada, Alcoholic beverage taxation and control policies, 5th International Survey.

the modernization and urbanization beginning in the mid-1950s (M. Tri-mani, personal communication, 1982). The snack bar sells bottled mineral water, sandwiches, sweets, ice-cream, and sundry goods such as shampoo and razor blades. The most common drink consumed on-premises is espresso coffee. Unlike the inn, there are often no places to sit in a snack bar and the presence of women is accepted. In the summer, a few tables and chairs grace the outside of the bar for people to sit at leisure to drink their coffee in the morning, or their aperitif in the late afternoon. The modern snack bar in Italy, then, has been integrated into society to serve the newly industrialized working class. As workers moved to the cities, took industrial jobs, and improved their standard of living to the point where they had comfortable homes to spend time in, the inn no longer served a necessary function. The snack bar, on the other hand, fits well into a modern urban industrial lifestyle.

A medical problem
If abstaining was regarded with indifference by the mid-1950s, so were issues of crime or social control connected to alcohol problems. The issues of intoxication, disinhibition, social defence, and concern over the urban proletariat that so occupied the scientific community in the nineteenth century were largely absent in the early 1950s. Although this was a time of tremendous instability in Italian society, characterized by rapid migration and urbanization, the prevailing scientific view was that alcoholism was principally a physiological dependence, rather than a cultural or psycho-logical problem.

In fact, Jellinek *(7)* reported that psychotherapy was quickly giving way to drug-oriented treatment, chiefly involving the use of disulfiram or apo-morphine. Although noting a cautionary trend on the part of members of the clinical community, he also reported that " paradoxically, it has aroused more interest in the psychotherapy of alcoholics than had been evidenced previous to the use of those drugs". Jellinek noted that in the 1950s alcoholic psychosis was the principal definition for alcoholism, used by both public and professionals. Thus, he noted:

> In the absence of the criterion of alcoholic psychosis the excessive drinker is re-garded as an occasional drunkard, or he may be overlooked entirely as a certain proportion of Italian alcoholics may develop adaptation to — and dependence upon — alcohol without showing outward symptoms of intoxication.

It is important to recognize that the same attitudes generally prevail today.

Issues of social control did not, however, disappear entirely; instead, they took on a more sophisticated medical cast. During the period of Italy's most intense postwar modernization, the Government sponsored several research projects on the effects of alcohol on worker productivity, absentee-ism and work-related injuries *(8,9)*. In addition, alcohol control laws were modified in 1949, 1953, 1971 and 1974, chiefly relating to licensing concerns.

Although there have been some changes in alcohol problem indicators, and although health system reforms have had an impact on treatment, there is a pervasive narrowness of both problem definition and treatment alternatives. A treatment system oriented towards drug therapy and established within the mental health community has characterized most of the postwar period. Admissions to mental hospitals for alcoholism continued to rise throughout the 1960s and 1970s. Significantly, however, admissions for alcoholic psychosis began levelling off in the 1960s, and declined in the 1970s.[a] Since no national study of alcohol problems has been undertaken to date in Italy, the explanation for this decline is open to speculation.

The 1978 mental health reform law, which provided for the deinstitutionalization of mental health care by closing the large asylums and creating community outpatient services, has effectively eliminated treatment for alcoholism from the public mental health units. People with alcohol problems are now either limited to detoxification wards at general hospitals (temporary care units primarily overcrowded with drug, not alcohol, overdose problems) or are treated in private hospitals. It is the traditional psychiatric service, however, that has remained in control, so that alcoholics are still awaiting the completion of mental health and psychiatric reform programmes. Since, therefore, the alcoholic now receives less help than before, he has become increasingly visible, a trend that has helped to stimulate renewed calls for a return to a separatist approach (F. Prina, unpublished observations, 1983). This is resulting in a prolonged and bitter debate among the national political parties. Thus, political party conflict, which frames health care policy in general, is shaping the current and future patterns of alcohol treatment.

The wine industry

Moreover, the tremendous growth of the wine industry in Italy has also brought a correspondingly strong state interest in the minimization of alcohol problems. Italy's role in the European Community and its attempt to compete in the world market-place in several commodity areas has deeply affected the marketing of alcoholic drinks both domestically and internationally. Internally, more foreign brands, especially of spirits and beer, are now available on the domestic market. Internationally, the Italian alcoholic drinks market has been shaped both by the entry of foreign capital into domestic production, and by changes in the export and import market. These changes in the economic significance of wine production might account for the continuing narrow definition of alcohol problems.

In 1978, Italy was the tenth largest importer of alcohol in the world with 3% of the world market at a value of US $86 million. In the same year, Italy ranked third in the world for alcohol exports with 11% of the world market valued at US $721 million. The export market chiefly consists of wine, with 19% of the world exports valued at US $675 million.

Italy, which is at the heart of the wine-producing centre of the world, today produces and exports more wine than any other country. With a

---

[a] **Vetere, C.** *Recent statistical elements concerning the prevalence of alcoholism in Italy.* (Unpublished working paper prepared for the US Department of Health, Education, and Welfare, 1978).

continuing growth in wine production and a decrease in domestic wine consumption, Italy, like France and Spain, has had to expand its export market to help shrink the "wine lake" that has grown in Europe. Overproduction has kept prices on both the European and the Italian domestic markets low. In Italy, for example, although the prices double or even treble between producers and consumers *(10)*, the average retail price of table wine in 1980/1981 was around 2000 lire per litre (roughly US $1.50) *(11)*. Overproduction has also strained the capacity of the cellars to store the fermenting wine. This problem is not new to the European Community. In 1974/1975, the bumper harvest of the previous two years forced the distilling of over 20 million hl of table wine, while another 16.8 million hl were put in storage *(12)*. In 1979, the volume of unsold wine amounted to over 35 million hl *(13)*.

As little as six years ago, experts were predicting vast problems in the European wine market owing to increased planting in the wine countries, the levelling off of consumption in those countries, and the lack of new markets opening up *(14)*. Italy, after France, seemed to be faring especially badly: first, because the growth in the production of wine seemed to be organized less according to what the wine market could take and more around building up economic growth in certain sectors of the country; and second, because the wine sector in Italy remained very decentralized, with little coordination among regions.

Nevertheless, the Italian wine sector seems to have surmounted some of these difficulties with a big growth in exports, especially to the United States, where Italy now controls over 61% of total wine imports compared with only 18.4% in 1970 *(15)*. Of the top 50 branded wines imported in the United States, 23 are Italian, representing 149.9 million cases out of a total of 160.2 million cases. The entry of large foreign investment into the Italian alcohol market has already had some impact on the domestic structure of distribution and production. Moreover, it is a catalyst for the increased expansion and internationalization of the productive structure.

Modernization programmes and cooperative holding companies are at least partly a result of these factors. The entry of large foreign firms has also sharpened competition. Italy has begun to alter federal policy and federal subsidy programmes to support those wine industries that compete best on the foreign market. This, in turn, has contributed to the state's economic interest in alcohol as a commodity and also to the continuing neglect of alcohol-related problems.

Conclusions

In Chapter 2, Mäkelä pointed out that there is a general tendency in most European countries today for the focus in alcohol control to move from the bottle to the man. In the case of Italy, this is only partially true, since today's more liberal legislation (compared to the Fascist and pre-Fascist periods) is evidence that Italy has almost completely neglected alcohol-related problems. Even the most sociopolitical legislation pays hardly any attention to the alcohol question. Among the 104 articles that make up the 1975 law on the control of opiates and psychotropic substances, only *one* article mentions alcohol.

It must be concluded that the public, which now sees drug addiction as a social problem, views alcoholism as an essentially personal problem. The implication of this view is contained in the statement by Terzian, that "nothing can be done to prevent such an inherently human evil; that the only possible response is a careful study of the direct or indirect physical or psychological damage caused by drink, in the hope of investigating its effects by shorter or longer periods of medical treatment or internment in hospitals or psychiatric institutions" *(16)*.

In summary, therefore, there are three phases to the Italian alcohol question: a phase of protocapitalism; a totalitarian phase; and a welfare phase. The alcohol question, having been initially defined mainly in social terms, then became defined in medical and law and order terms, and has now been redefined as an individual, personal problem. It is indeed the drug problem that currently dominates Italian legal, political and cultural thinking.

Nevertheless, the alcohol problem also requires attention. There should be increasing emphasis on its social, economic and political aspects; some fundamental distinctions (between urban and rural contexts; between North and South; between various social classes) should be investigated; and, finally, special attention should be paid to those situations where changes in drinking patterns and in their significance are most likely to occur.

References

1. **Cottino, A.** Instinct or milieu: the alcoholic question from Lombroso to Ferri. *In: Sociologi i brytningstid, sociologiska institutionen.* Umeå, Umeå Universitet, 1983.
2. **Colajanni, N.** *L'alcolismo, sue consequenze morali, sue cause.* Catania, Tropea, 1882.
3. **Lombroso, C.** Il vino nel delitto. *In: Il Vino.* Turin, Loescher, 1880.
4. **Cherrington, E.H., ed.** *Standard encylopedia of the alcohol problem.* 1926, Vol. 3.
5. **de Grazia, V.** *The culture of consent: mass organization of leisure in Fascist Italy.* Cambridge, Cambridge University Press, 1981.
6. **Guerri, G.B., ed.** *B. Bottai: Diary 1935–1944.* Milan, Rizzoli, 1982.
7. **Jellinek, E.M.** Italy. *In:* Popham, R.E., ed. *Jellinek working papers on drinking patterns and alcohol problems.* Toronto, Addiction Research Foundation, 1976.
8. **Mangano, M. & Mangano, M.G.** *L'alcoolismo e i suio reflessi sul lavoro* [Alcoholism and its effects on work]. Rome, Istituto Italiano di Medicina Sociale, 1969.
9. **D'Arca, S.U. et al.** *Indagine sull'alcoolismo in una collettività lavorativa* [Study on alcoholism in a working community]. Rome, Istituto Italiano di Medicina Sociale, 1970.
10. *Marketing in Europe,* No. 203 (1970).
11. *Ivram informazione,* No. 88 (1982).

12. *Marketing in Europe,* No. 182 (1978).
13. *Marketing in Europe,* No. 218 (1981).
14. *Studio sull'evoluzione della concentrazione nell'industria delle bevande in Italia* [Study on the growth of concentration in the drinks industry in Italy]. Brussels, Commission of the European Communities, 1976.
15. *Impact,* 1 March 1981.
16. **Terzian, H.** La cultura della vigna e del vino [Vineyards and wine]. *In: Patologia e problemi connessi all'uso inadeguato di alcoolici* [Pathology and problems connected with the poor habits of alcoholics]. Giunta Regionale del Veneto, 1982 (Quaderni di educazione sanitaria).

Greece — *J.N. Yfantopoulos*

World statistics show that the production of alcoholic drinks has been increasing since the Second World War.[a] From a sample of 177 countries in 6 areas of the world, data for the period 1960–1972 indicate that the production of wine increased by 19%, of spirits by 61% and of beer by 68%.

In Greece, alcoholic drinks production represents 2.6% of the national gross domestic product. The beer industry has the largest share (40%), followed by wine (32%) and spirits (28%). Alcohol production accounts for 58% of the labour force working in the production of soft drinks and alcoholic drinks. Of the various sectors of the alcohol industry, the labour force in the beer industry receives the highest wages. In 1977, the annual disposable income per employee in each sector of the alcohol industry was estimated to be:

— beer industry: 219 800 drachmae
— spirits industry: 187 900 drachmae
— wine industry: 167 600 drachmae

The relatively higher wages in the beer industry can be attributed to its fast growth rate and to increased investments in this sector. The increasing need for more specialized personnel, as well as better organizational and administrative structures in this sector, have contributed to a better and more efficient use of resources.

The wine industry

Domestic wine production amounts to 500 000 tonnes per year, which is 3.5% of the total production of the European Economic Community (EEC) countries and 1.5% of world production. About two thirds of Greek wine is produced by industrialized or semi-industrialized processes. Although 80% of total EEC production is in the form of red wine, in Greece red wine makes up only 40% of total production.

---

[a] *Alcohol consumption and alcohol-related problems: development of national policies and programmes* (unpublished WHO document A35/Technical Discussions/1, 1982).

The production of wine is seriously influenced by a number of factors such as weather conditions, crop diseases, methods of cultivation and collection of grapes, and available means of transport. Wine requires a clear sequential process for its production and distribution. There are relatively few agricultural cooperatives in Greece, with the result that individual farmers are responsible for producing and distributing their own products. Table 1 shows the annual output of the wine industry for the period 1975–1980.

Table 1. Annual output of the wine industry, 1975–1980

Year	Output (thousand tonnes)	Annual change (%)
1975	451	—
1976	500	+ 10.9
1977	473	− 5.4
1978	508	+ 7.4
1979	482	− 5.1
1980	522	+ 8.3

Source: Ministry of Health and Welfare.

Table 2 shows the wholesale prices for white and red wines for the period 1977–1980. Up to 1979 white wine was more expensive than red, but after 1980, when the production process was brought into line with European standards, the quality of red wine improved substantially, thus leading to a price increase.

Table 2. Wholesale prices for red and white wines, 1977–1980

Year	Price per litre (drachmae)	
	Red wine	White wine
1977	73.9	78.6
1978	70.4	81.5
1979	82.6	100.5
1980	134.4	116.9

Source: Ministry of Health and Welfare.

Regardless of the place of production, a duty of 6.76 drachmae per kilogram is levied on all wine products. In addition the following taxes are

Regardless of the place of production, a duty of 6.76 drachmae per kilogram is levied on all wine products. In addition the following taxes are levied:

— 40% of the value (since wine is considered a luxury item)

— 3–4% of the value as stamp duties

— 15 drachmae per kilogram as consumption tax.

The beer industry

During 1981/1982 there was a remarkable increase in beer production. Total production capacity increased by 70–80%, which implies a possible increase of 3 640 000 hl per year. There is a long-term plan in the beer industry to improve the utilization of existing resources. Table 3 shows the annual production of the Greek beer industry for the period 1974–1980, revealing an impressive increase over time.

According to Law No. 72 of 1977, the price of beer is under government control. A fixed profit for every stage of production has been specified and includes a 5% surcharge on the cost of production and a 20% surcharge on the transport cost.

Beer is subject to a consumption tax only, which is levied at the rate of 55 drachmae per kilogram.

Table 3. Annual output of the beer industry, 1974–1980

Year	Output (thousand hl)	Annual change (%)
1974	1484.5	—
1975	1341.4	– 9.6
1976	1374.4	+ 2.5
1977	1798.6	+30.9
1978	1992.0	+10.8
1979	2462.0	+23.6
1980	2535.0	+ 3.0

Source: Ministry of Health and Welfare.

The spirits industry

The spirits industry in Greece functions under strict government control. It includes 17 producers, all of which are based in the Athens area. Their annual production capacity is estimated to be 51 000 tonnes of pure alcohol,

94

but spirit production in 1979 was 33 950 tonnes, an indication of the relatively low level of utilization of the existing capacity. The existing capital equipment is rather old and there have been few modern technological advances. Estimates of the production trends in spirits are shown in Table 4.

Table 4. Annual output of the spirits industry, 1974–1979

Year	Output (tonnes)	Annual change (%)
1974	25 950	—
1975	23 605	− 9.0
1976	27 267	+15.5
1977	28 188	+ 3.4
1978	32 102	+13.9
1979	33 950	+ 5.8

Source: Ministry of Health and Welfare.

The wholesale price of alcohol is under government control, the price being set annually by the Ministry of Finance. In April 1981, the following prices per litre were specified:

— 125 drachmae for spirits

— 115.5 drachmae for pure alcohol (95%).

On pure alcohol, a tax of 55.2 drachmae per kilogram is levied, while for all other spirits the following alcohol duty is levied:

— a consumption tax of 15 drachmae per kilogram

— 40% duty

— 5.2% stamp duty.

Consumption trends

Macro analysis
In the decade 1970–1980, the average annual growth in the consumption of alcoholic drinks was 18.6%. The corresponding rate for total private consumption was 18.9% and that of national income was 19.3%. At the same time the number of tourists who visited Greece increased at an annual rate of 11.1% and the foreign exchange imported per tourist increased at a rate of 7.8%. Comparing these increases, it is clear that tourists played an important role in the consumption of alcohol products. Owing to the lack of

95

reliable data it is not possible to estimate precisely what proportion of total alcohol consumption can be attributed to tourists. On the basis of some general estimates, however, an attempt will be made to analyse the consumption trends of wine, beer and spirits (see Fig. 1).

Fig. 1. Yearly *per capita* consumption of wine, beer and spirits, 1970–1980[a]

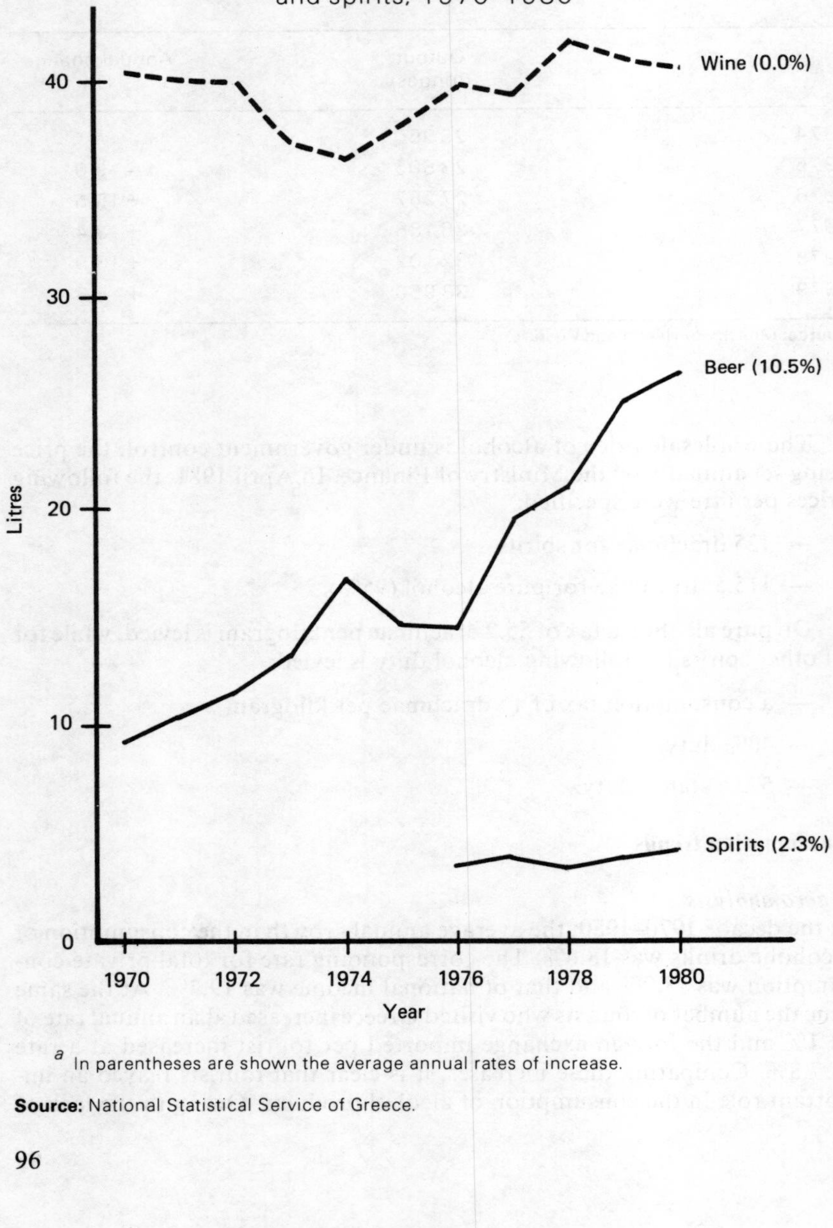

[a] In parentheses are shown the average annual rates of increase.

Source: National Statistical Service of Greece.

Consumption of wine. The *per capita* consumption of wine is estimated to amount to about 40 litres per year. In comparison with many other European countries, the Greek consumption of wine is rather low.[a] The Greek consumer preferences for different types of wine can be analysed as follows:

Domestic wine	73%
Very high quality wine	23%
Imported wine	4%

Consumption of beer. During the period 1972–1980 there was an impressive increase in the consumption of beer, at an average annual rate of 11.7%. The main factors that influenced this increase can be summarized as follows:

— new factories for beer were established and new types of beer were introduced;

— the price of beer was relatively low in comparison with the prices of other alcohol products; and

— the number of tourists increased and it is estimated that tourists consume a large quantity of beer every year.

Beer is consumed mainly by the younger generations (Fig. 2). By 1988, annual *per capita* consumption of beer is expected to reach 40 litres.

Consumption of spirits. The *per capita* consumption of spirits has remained steady, amounting to about 4 litres per year. It has been estimated that the main consumers of spirits are among the higher income groups.

Consumption trends and economic policy. A number of researchers *(1)* have used different econometric models to obtain estimates for two very significant parameters for economic policies, namely income and price elasticities. Elasticity is a useful parameter for economic policy purposes, because it provides important information on the relative sensitivity of two variables, by measuring the proportional increase (or decrease) of an independent variable and showing its proportional impact on a dependent variable. Thus, elasticities provide information on, say, a 10% increase in price or in income, and measure how such increases might influence the demand for alcoholic drinks.

---

[a] *Alcohol consumption and alcohol-related problems: development of national policies and programmes* (unpublished WHO document A35/Technical Discussions/1, 1982).

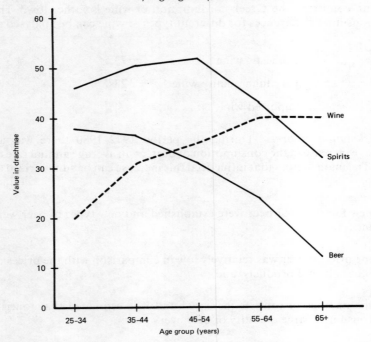

Fig. 2. Monthly expenditure on alcoholic drinks,
by age group in 1974

Value in drachmae

Wine

Spirits

Beer

25-34   35-44   45-54   55-64   65+

Age group (years)

Source: National Statistical Service of Greece (household survey, 1974).

Different econometric models have been used for estimating these two
parameters, but the most popular is the double logarithmic model, which
can be expressed either in an exponential or a logarithmic form.

Exponential: $D_i = A Y^{\alpha_1} P_i^{\alpha_2}$

Logarithmic: $\log D_i = \log A + \alpha_1 \log Y + \alpha_2 \log P_i$

where D_i = the demand for alcoholic drinks (i) which may be beer,
         wine or spirits

A = constant term

Y = income

P_i = price for the drink, i (beer, wine or spirits)

α_1 = income elasticity

α_2 = price elasticity

Table 5 shows the elasticities that have been estimated in the empirical
literature for different alcoholic drinks.

Table 5. Price and income elasticities for various alcoholic drinks

Study	Drink	Elasticities	
		Price	Income
Stone & Rowe (1958)	Beer	-0.53	0.68
	Other drinks	1.52	3.23
Rowe (1965)	All drinks and	-0.69 (1900)	1.54
	tobacco	-0.26 (1938)	1.23
		-0.18 (1960)	0.74
Central Statistical	Beer	-0.2	0.7
Office (1980)	Wine	-1.1	2.5
	Spirits	-1.6	2.2
Duffy (1980)	Beer	Insignificant	0.8 to 1.1
	Wine	-0.65 to -0.87	
	Spirits	-0.8 to -1.0	1.6

Source: Maynard & Kennan. P. *(1)*.

As far as Greece is concerned, various models have been used for estimating price and income elasticities. One study by Bartholomaios *(2)* on price elasticities for all alcoholic drinks showed the following results: using a static model the price elasticity was – 5.11, and using a dynamic model it was – 1.81 in the short run, and – 3.69 in the long run. For estimating income elasticities in the present study the following model was used: $D = AY^{\alpha_1}$, where D is the demand for all alcoholic drinks, A is a constant term, α_1 is the income elasticity and Y is the income. The result was $D = 6.12\,Y^{1.20}$. In logarithmic form this model was:

$$\log D = 6.12 + 1.2 \log Y \qquad\qquad R^2 = 0.94$$
$$(3.53)$$

The t ratios are shown in parentheses. R^2 represents the coefficient of determination that shows the goodness of fit. The closer R^2 is to 1, the better the fit. Hence, the estimated income elasticity is 1.2, which means that a 10% increase in income would increase the total consumption of all alcoholic drinks by 12%.

Micro analysis
This section focuses on household consumption patterns analysing Greek consumption preferences for alcohol products, and attempting to estimate income elasticities for beer, wine, spirits and for all alcoholic drinks. A study

is also made of the relationship between alcohol consumption and professional groups, age, urban/rural population and unemployment.

The micro analysis of alcohol consumption patterns in Greece is based on a household survey carried out in 1974 by the National Statistical Service of Greece, covering both urban and rural populations. On average in 1974 the monthly expenditure on alcohol products of a representative Greek household amounted to 157 drachmae, which equals 1.6% of the total household budget (see Table 6). The consumption of beer and wine accounts for lower *per capita* expenditure than that of spirits. An interesting figure with an important social implication is the consumption of alcohol products outside the house, in a tavern, bar or restaurant. This shows, as will be argued later, that alcohol consumption in Greece includes some important psychosocial aspects of socialization, which should be clearly distinguished from alcoholism.

Table 6. Average monthly expenditures on alcohol products in 1974

	Monthly expenditure in drachmae		Percentage of household budget
	Per household	*Per capita*	
Alcohol consumption at home:			
Wine	32	9	0.3
Beer	29	9	0.3
Spirits	45	13	0.5
Alcohol consumption outside the home	51	15	0.5
Total alcohol consumption	157	46	1.6

Source: National Statistical Service of Greece (household survey, 1974).

Income and alcohol consumption. The relationship between income and alcohol consumption is very important for economic policy purposes. As income rises, it is interesting to know both what proportion of this increase will be devoted to alcohol consumption and what type of alcoholic drink will be consumed. From Table 7 it can be seen that as income increases, expenditure on alcoholic drinks also increases, but not at the same rate for all products. By estimating the income elasticities for various alcohol products (see Table 8), it becomes clear that beer and spirits have elasticities very close

Table 7. Average monthly expenditure per household on alcohol products, by income group, in 1974

Income group (monthly income in drachmae)	Monthly expenditure in drachmae on:				
	total alcohol consumption	alcohol consumption at home			alcohol consumption outside the home
		Wine	Beer	Spirits	
0– 999	9	1	1	3	4
1 000– 1 999	30	7	3	11	9
2 000– 2 999	60	15	5	19	21
3 000– 4 999	96	19	16	22	39
5 000– 6 999	132	23	18	38	53
7 000– 9 999	146	34	24	37	51
10 000–13 999	201	43	42	53	63
14 000–19 999	239	55	47	55	82
20 000–29 999	300	58	77	97	68
30 000 +	452	46	84	232	90
All income groups (average)	157	32	29	45	51

Source: National Statistical Service of Greece (household survey, 1974).

to 1. This means that a 10% increase in income would increase the consumption of these products by the same percentage (10.1% for beer and 9.4% for spirits). The income elasticities were estimated using the following model:

$$D_i = AY^{\alpha_3}$$

where D_i = expenditure on different alcohol products

Y = income

α_3 = income elasticity

A = constant term

The results obtained using this model are as follows. R^2 represents the coefficient of determination that shows the goodness of fit of the estimated regression. The closer R^2 is to 1, the better the fit.

Table 8. Income elasticities: per cent changes in consumption of alcohol products resulting from a 10% increase in income

	Total alcohol consumption	Alcohol consumption at home			Alcohol consumption outside the home
		Wine	Beer	Spirits	
Increase in the consumption of alcohol products (%)	9.8	7.7	10.1	9.4	7.4
Estimated income elasticities (double logarithmic functions)	0.98	0.77	1.01	0.94	0.74

Total alcohol consumption $= -3.48\ Y^{0.98}$ $\qquad R^2 = 0.44$

Consumption at home:

$\qquad$ Wine $= -3.69\ Y^{0.77}$ $\qquad R^2 = 0.88$

$\qquad$ Beer $= -5.95\ Y^{1.01}$ $\qquad R^2 = 0.96$

$\qquad$ Spirits $= -4.74\ Y^{0.94}$ $\qquad R^2 = 0.98$

Consumption outside the home $= -2.98\ Y^{0.74}$ $\qquad R^2 = 0.88$

Professional groups and alcohol consumption. Considering the alcohol consumption patterns of different professional groups (see Table 9) it becomes clear that:

— wine is mainly consumed by agricultural workers and technicians;

— beer is preferred by those working in the private and public sectors, including civil servants;

— spirits are mainly consumed by scientists, businessmen, and managers.

Finally, it is interesting to note that agricultural workers, technicians and businessmen are the professions that show the greatest interest in drinking outside the home.

Age and alcohol consumption. Fig. 2 shows how alcohol consumption increases with age, up to the age of 55, when it starts to decrease again. It also

Table 9. Average monthly expenditure per household on alcohol products, by professional group, in 1974

| Professional group | Monthly expenditure in drachmae on: | | | | |
| | total alcohol consumption | alcohol consumption at home | | | alcohol consumption outside the home |
		Wine	Beer	Spirits	
Scientists	147	20	39	71	17
Managers	149	25	32	63	29
Civil servants	146	31	42	47	26
Businessmen	191	28	35	65	63
Service providers	103	32	15	27	29
Agricultural workers	222	39	33	54	96
Technicians	172	38	31	42	61
Unemployed	94	23	19	31	21
Average	157	32	29	45	51

Source: National Statistical Service of Greece (household survey, 1974).

shows the preferences of different groups for wine, spirits and beer, and clearly illustrates the old Greek proverb that "wine is the milk of old people". The younger age groups show a preference for spirits and beer but for both of these products wine is substituted as age increases.

Alcohol consumption patterns in urban and rural populations. Estimates for the relative consumption patterns of urban and rural populations are based on two studies. The first was a household survey undertaken by the National Statistical Service of Greece in 1974 and the second was a study undertaken by Karapostolis in 1979 *(3).*

From these studies, it emerges that the *per capita* consumption of alcohol and tobacco products increased in the decade 1964–1974 in both urban (165%) and rural (316%) populations. As can be seen from the expenditure elasticities (Table 10), however, while the demand for alcohol and tobacco products increased in urban populations (increase in elasticities from 0.73 in 1964 to 1.01 in 1974) it decreased in rural populations (decline in elasticities from 0.98 in 1964 to 0.89 in 1974). In addition, the percentage of the household budget that was devoted to the consumption of these products fell in rural populations from 6.9% to 6.1% and remained stable at 3.9% in

Table 10. Consumption of alcohol and tobacco products in urban and rural populations

Population	Percentage of household budget spent		Expenditure elasticity	
	1964	1974	1964	1974
Urban	3.9	3.9	0.73	1.01
Rural	6.9	6.1	0.98	0.89

the urban populations throughout the decade. From another study, it appears that annual discharge rates from hospitals are much higher in urban areas than in rural areas for alcohol-related disabilities, though in both populations the rates are increasing (Table 11). The overall rate of illness attributable to alcohol is nevertheless considered to be very low in comparison with other European countries with similar levels of alcohol consumption.

In relation to the consumption of alcohol and tobacco in urban and rural populations, it is interesting to study some psychosocial aspects of drinking, especially whether drinking takes place at home or outside. From the two studies mentioned, it emerges that the percentage of the household budget spent on drinking outside the home in a social place (such as a tavern or restaurant that also serves food or snacks) is much higher in the rural areas

Table 11. Annual discharge rates per 100 000 population for alcohol-related disabilities from all hospitals (including psychiatric hospitals and clinics)

Region	1975	1977
Urban:		
Athens	13.3	21.8
Piraeus	8.7	8.5
Salonica	8.7	18.9
Rural	3.37	3.83

Source: Liakos, A. et al. *Alcohol consumption and rates of alcoholism in Greece: drug and alcohol dependence,* Vol. 6. 1980, pp. 425–430.

than in the urban areas (Table 12). This finding illustrates the conventional type of lifestyle in rural areas, where people tend to gather together in taverns where they also drink together. Drinking is considered a social event and not an alcoholic habit. Epidemiological studies by Blum & Blum *(4)* have shown that Greece does not have a pronounced problem of alcoholism for this very reason.

Table 12. Percentage of household budget spent
on alcohol products, every month,
by type of drink and population

Population	Alcohol consumption at home			Alcohol consumption outside the home
	Wine	Beer	Spirits	
Urban	0.3	0.2	0.4	0.3
Semi-urban	0.3	0.3	0.6	0.8
Rural	0.6	0.5	0.7	1.2

Source: National Statistical Service of Greece (household survey, 1974).

Unemployment and alcohol consumption. The relationship between unemployment and alcohol consumption is controversial since there appears to be empirical evidence that the relationship between these two issues could be both positive and negative.

A positive association has been found in the Nordic countries supporting the hypothesis that the higher the rate of unemployment in a country, the greater the social and family problems and the higher the frustration of the individual. It is possible that one solution to this situation would be to consume more alcohol, although this has not been demonstrated.

During the 1930s, however, when the economic crisis was at its peak, a negative association between unemployment and alcohol consumption was observed, suggesting that lack of spending power reduced the consumption of most goods that were considered inessential, including alcohol. Similar trends are emerging from studies currently being undertaken in Scotland. Since other factors such as culture, religious beliefs, and differences in drinking behaviour need to be taken into account, great caution should be exercised in interpreting these data.

The Greek data (see Table 9) suggest that the unemployed spend much less on alcohol in comparison with others, thus supporting the hypothesis of a negative association between unemployment and alcohol consumption.

Tourism and alcohol consumption

Tourism is considered to be one of the main sources of economic development in Greece. The demand for tourist services has been increasing steadily for the last decade in most southern European countries (Table 13). This demand is influenced by many factors including the exchange rate, the relative prices of tourist services offered in other countries and the social, cultural and economic development of the country.

Table 13. Tourist arrivals in the Mediterranean area, 1975–1980

Area	Arrivals (millions)		Average annual rate of increase	
	1975	1980	1960–1975 (%)	1975–1980 (%)
North-west Mediterranean	88.8	108.0	7.7	4.0
North-east Mediterranean: Greece, Turkey, Yugoslavia	10.5	16.9	13.9	10.0
Algeria, Morocco	2.1	5.2	16.5	20.0
Cyprus, Egypt, Israel	3.2	4.5	13.2	7.0
Total	104.6	134.6	8.4	5.6

Source: Centre of Planning and Economic Research.

Greek statistics reveal (see Table 14) that since 1975 the number of tourists has increased rapidly. This may be attributed both to better organization of tourist services and to substantial improvements in the availability of hotel beds and similar services. The average annual rate of increase in hotel beds is estimated to have been 8% from 1960 to 1967 and 10% from 1968 to 1978.

Other factors include general increases in wealth and improvements in the management of mass tourism. As modern life becomes increasingly stressful, holidays are regarded as more and more essential. According to some Greek estimates, the income elasticity for tourist services is close to 1.

Despite the rapid expansion of hotel and tourist services, the future development of the tourist industry in Greece is not expected to be as flourishing as in recent years. As can be seen from Table 14, the average annual rate of growth in tourist arrivals to Greece is expected to fall from

Table 14. Tourist arrivals in Greece, 1975–1985

Arrivals (thousands)			Average annual rate of growth	
1975	1980	1985[a]	1976–1980 (%)	1981–1985[a] (%)
2643	4750	6350–7000	12.5	6–8

[a] Estimate.

Source: Centre of Planning and Economic Research.

12.5% in 1976–1980 to about 7% in 1981–1985. This projected decline may be attributed to current economic problems, such as inflation, reduction in real income and increase in unemployment. This reduction in tourist arrivals will influence the various economic trends in the country, including patterns of alcohol consumption.

A study on alcohol consumption among tourists
The only attempt to assess the consumption patterns of tourists in Greece was made by the National Tourist Organization in the summer of 1970. The main reasons for the failure to repeat this study may be attributed to a number of factors such as difficulties in estimating the exact number of tourists in any given period, in obtaining reliable responses, and in designing a representative sample. There was also a lack of appropriate personnel with multilingual abilities and of the required funds. The 1970 study should therefore be considered only as an attempt to obtain some very general information.

The sample. In the summer of 1970, a small number of researchers at Hellinicon Airport interviewed a randomly selected number of tourists. After briefing, a questionnaire with 12 basic questions was given to the selected tourists, who were asked to complete it while staying in Greece. Various incentives, including participation in a lottery, were offered to encourage a response. In all, 1200 questionnaires were distributed and only 141 were returned, covering 250 tourists, of whom 220 were on vacation, 10 were on business, 14 were visiting friends and 6 were passing through Greece on their way to another country. The sample consisted of Americans (40%), Germans (12%), French (6%), English (5%) and various other nationalities (37%).

The results. Statistical analysis revealed that 4.65% of the budget of the average tourist was spent on alcohol products. English and Australian

107

people spent a relatively higher proportion of their budget (7.07% and 6.21% respectively) on alcohol products than Americans, who appeared to be the lowest consumers with 2.4%. Of course, great care should be exercised in interpreting these findings owing to all the difficulties mentioned above, as well as to the possible low standards of reliability and comparability. Unfortunately, the tourists were not asked whether they preferred beer to wine or spirits. Surveys indicate, however, that most tourists prefer Greek wine to beer. For the time being, we do not have sufficient data to support any hypotheses regarding the drinking patterns of tourists in Greece, and the results of the 1970 study should be considered only as an exercise with potential for future improvement.

National Greek policies

Health education programmes
Since Greece is a wine-producing country where the wine industry contributes significantly to the gross domestic product of the country, a co-ordinated health education programme has not been adopted. In addition, because of the low incidence of alcoholism, there has not been the need, so far, to develop health education campaigns against alcohol products.

Health legislation
Various legislative acts have been introduced in Greece at different times with regard to alcohol consumption. The first of these, Act No. 992, was passed in 1971 prohibiting the sale of alcoholic drinks to anyone under 18 years of age. The same legislation defines the working hours of all bars and public houses as well as the conditions for selling alcohol products. In 1979 this law was reconsidered and the conditions for selling alcoholic drinks were changed by Act No. 180.

Article 42 of Act No. 614, passed in 1977, prohibits driving with more than a certain level of alcohol in the blood. The Ministry of Transport and the Ministry of Justice have together specified the procedure that should be used to measure the level of alcohol in the blood of drivers.

According to figures provided by the Traffic Police the number of traffic accidents attributed to alcohol almost tripled between 1980 and 1981. Serious crimes attributed to alcoholism or heavy drinking have also risen steeply in recent years. The actual number of incidents is still very low, however.

The legislative acts that have been adopted are aimed at controlling crimes and traffic accidents attributed to heavy drinking. There has not been any legislation aimed at reducing general alcohol consumption, nor does there, for the time being, appear to be such a need to introduce an anti-alcohol campaign or any other severe measures for controlling alcoholism.

References
1. **Maynard, A. & Kennan, P.** The economics of alcohol abuse. *British journal of addiction,* **76**: 339–345 (1981).

2. **Bartholomaios, J.** *An analysis of demand for consumer products in Greece.* Spoudai, 1974, pp. 758–775.
3. **Karapostolis, B.** *Consumption patterns in the rural areas of Greece.* Athens, Agricultural Bank of Greece, 1979 (Series No. 8).
4. **Blum, H. & Blum, E.** Drinking practices and controls in rural Greece. *British journal of addiction,* **60**: 93–108 (1964).

Poland — *I. Wald, J. Morawski & J. Moskalewicz*

To understand the factors determining alcohol consumption and alcohol control in Poland, it is necessary to consider the features that distinguish Poland from other European countries. In the years 1945–1980, a notable economic development took place. Poland was transformed from a predominantly agricultural country into a predominantly industrial one. The national income increased 6.7 times over the period 1950–1978, while the proportion of the urban population rose from 37% in 1950 to 59% in 1981.

The end of the 1970s marked the beginning of a period of crisis in Poland. Starting from 1979 the national income began to decrease. Assuming a value in 1978 of 100, it fell to 97.7 in 1979, 91.8 in 1980, and 80.8 in 1981. The summer of 1980 brought a wave of strikes in Poland, leading to a change of government and then, on 13 December 1981, to the introduction of martial law. Although this was lifted on 31 December 1982, Poland still remains in a state of economic and social crisis *(1)*.

Drinking habits

Poland is one of the countries in which the Scandinavian model of alcohol consumption prevails. This model is typified by the concentrated consumption of large quantities of drinks. In the years 1950–1980, alcohol consumption in Poland increased quite rapidly, as is clear from Fig. 1 which shows alcohol consumption in the years 1950–1982. The early part of this period saw the declining share of spirits in total consumption, a trend that was halted in 1964, since when the share of vodka in consumption has increased again. As in many other European countries, tendencies that were noted during this period have included a decreasing number of abstainers in the general population, increasing alcohol consumption among women, substantial increases in drinking among youth, and more frequent drinking in the workplace *(2)*. As alcohol problems became more visible, so they began to be rated by public opinion as among the most severe problems of the country *(3)*.

Alcohol control

Issues of alcohol control have always been the concern of the state. The production of spirits has long been a state monopoly, and since the Second World War virtually all alcoholic drinks have been produced by state and cooperative enterprises, which also play a dominant part in distribution. The most rigorous control regulations have traditionally concerned spirits;

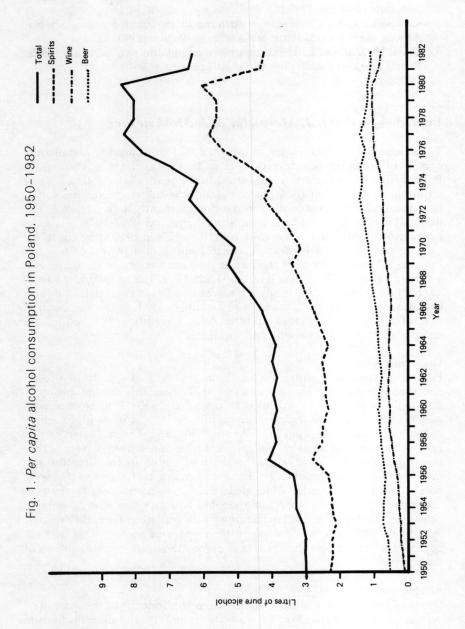

Fig. 1. *Per capita* alcohol consumption in Poland, 1950–1982

those concerning wine are less strict and those concerning beer are negligible, since beer is treated practically in the same way as all other alimentary goods. In 1956 and 1959 new laws were introduced on the prevention of alcoholism, including the decriminalization of public drunkenness, the establishment of sobering-up stations and the introduction of a new system for the treatment of alcoholism, with particular emphasis on compulsory treatment. The 1959 Law introduced various restrictions on the sale of alcoholic drinks such as licensed premises, licensing hours and minimum age limits for purchase (wine and vodka could only be sold to those of 18 years of age or over). The Law also incorporated the possibility of local options with regard to restrictions on alcohol sales.

Alcohol prices and rationing

Between 1950 and 1982, there were 13 increases in alcohol prices, most of which were followed by a temporary stabilization or even decrease in consumption. In 1972 and 1978, new resolutions were passed by the Council of Ministers to make alcohol control more rigorous. After the 1978 increase in alcohol prices, consumption stabilized for two years. In 1980, however, it rose again to a level of 8.4 litres of pure alcohol equivalent per head of population.

One symptom of the increasing crises in Poland in 1981 was a breakdown in the alcohol market. Alcohol rationing was introduced as a result, first locally and then, in October 1981, nationally. Rationing allowed the sale of half a litre of vodka per month to everyone over 18, although alcohol sold on licensed premises was never rationed. Other products such as wine, sweets and coffee were available instead of vodka (within the so-called system of substitutes). In July 1982, with rationing still in force, free sales of alcohol at higher prices were allowed, in addition to the rations. In March 1983, the rationing of alcohol was lifted.

Although the rationing of alcohol brought about a drop in recorded consumption, it also raised the status of alcohol, widened the range of consumers, and increased the alcohol black market. As far as can be determined, there are now more illicit distillers in towns, most of them producing small quantities of alcohol, mainly based on sugar.

Government alcohol policy

The authorities have been particularly active in the field of alcohol control since 1981, when the government of General Jaruzelski included alcohol-related problems in its 10-point programme of action. This was followed by a number of moves, including a resolution concerning more rigorous enforcement of the restriction on the consumption of alcohol in the workplace. Activities of the government Commission for Alcohol Problems were intensified and preparation of a new alcohol law was started.

The 1982 Law

This bill was presented to the *Sejm* (Parliament) and passed on 26 October 1982 *(4)*. In contrast to the Law of 1959, the 1982 Law on upbringing in sobriety and counteracting alcoholism puts much more emphasis on prevention:

> The state administration bodies are obliged to undertake activities aimed to limit the consumption of alcoholic beverages; initiate and support actions aimed to change alcohol consumption patterns; propagate sobriety in the workplace; prevent and eliminate the consequences of excessive drinking and support activities in this field of voluntary organizations and institutions.

The Law proposes the formation and development of voluntary organizations to deal with alcohol-related problems and cooperation with the Catholic Church and religious organizations in the encouragement of sobriety and the prevention of alcoholism. It makes the Council of Ministers responsible for planning alcohol sales in such a way as to limit alcohol consumption. It also proposes the establishment of a separate state enterprise to deal with off-premises alcohol distribution and trade. Finally, increases in the price of alcoholic drinks should precede any rise in the income of the population.

The Law also imposes various information and educational tasks on particular ministries. The Commission for Alcohol Problems, chaired by one of Poland's deputy prime ministers, works as an advisory and coordinating body for the Council of Ministers with equivalent commissions operating at regional and local levels. Many restrictions on the accessibility of alcohol have been introduced, which are unlike those of 1959 in that they concern all alcoholic drinks (over 1.5% alcohol) including beer as well as wine and spirits. The Council of Ministers presents annual reports of their activities in the field of alcohol to the *Sejm,* while the heads of regional and local government must do the same to their respective national councils.

With regard to the treatment of alcoholism, the Law puts much more emphasis on voluntary treatment, widens the range of institutions that treat alcoholics including primary health care facilities, and departs from the system of compulsory treatment, introducing in its place a court obligation to apply for treatment.

The Law of 26 October 1982 actually came into force on 13 May 1983, together with about 20 executive acts that provide the basis for its implementation. This Law is intended as a step towards the preparation of a comprehensive alcohol policy. As early as 1981, the Expert Committee of the Council of Ministers' Commission for Alcohol Problems was asked to work out the guidelines of such a long-term policy. The document prepared by the Committee and presented to the government in 1982 contained the general outlines of an alcohol policy. A primary goal was the prevention and management of alcohol-related problems. Among the related objectives, special emphasis was given to the limiting of alcohol consumption and the modification of drinking patterns, by reducing the share of spirits in overall consumption.

Prerequisites
The document also describes the reprequisites for an effective alcohol policy. The policy should be of high validity, in the sense that its objectives

should be in line with those of general social policy, and it should be appropriate to the general conditions of society and its level of cultural development. It should be comprehensive, in the sense that it should take into account the fullest possible range of problems, and their causes and effects. It should be coherent, in the sense that it should avoid conflicting objectives, and it should be consistent, in the sense that it should not sacrifice its essential aims for the sake of those particular objectives. It should take into account information about the effects of various alcohol-related decisions made by the state. Finally, it should gain acceptance and active support from the community as a whole.

Constraints

All the activities described above are being carried out in a difficult social and economic climate, which imposes limitations on alcohol policy. There is no simple relationship, however, between the general situation and the opportunities that exist for implementing an alcohol policy. Thus, for example, a drop in the real income of the population reduces the demand for alcohol, while on the other hand, the lack of alternatives reduces the possibility of directing the demand elsewhere. Economic difficulties affect imports, thus limiting the range of possible changes in the alcohol consumption structure that could be achieved by importing grape wines. Moreover, there is a danger that the continuing economic crisis may result in fiscal concerns dominating social policy, thus introducing a conflict between the immediate and the long-term aims of the alcohol policy.

Conclusion

What has been presented here are the general lines of the Polish alcohol policy, with the new Law on alcohol as their essential element. Certain trends emerge for the future, but whether they can be accomplished will depend on many factors, including social and economic developments and particularly the active support of society.

References

1. **Wald, I. & Moskalewicz, J.** Alcohol policy in a crisis situation. *British journal of addiction,* **79**: 331–375 (1984).
2. **Wald, I. et al.** *Raport o problemach polityki w zakresie alkoholu* [Report on alcohol policy]. Warsaw, Instytut Wydawniczy Zwiazkow Zawodowych, 1981.
3. **Morawski, J.** Alcohol-related problems in Poland 1950–1981. *In:* Giesbrecht, N. et al., ed. *Consequences of drinking, trends in alcohol problem statistics in seven countries.* Toronto, Addiction Research Foundation, 1983.
4. **Poland.** Law of 26 October 1982 on education for sobriety and control of alcoholism. *Dziennik ustaw,* 12 December 1982, No. 5, pp. 625–630.

Sweden — *K.E. Bruun*

This section consists of a description of the history of the Swedish alcohol control systems, primarily based on a continuing research project on Swedish alcohol policies. The analysis relies on important investigations by Lenke *(1)* on the influence of controls on the distribution of consumption. Some historical studies are also important, including the work of Frånberg *(2)* and of Thulin & Marcus *(3)*. The studies by Lundkvist *(4)* into popular movements and by Åberg *(5)* into municipal policies at the turn of the century are also especially illuminating.

Alcohol control systems

An initial general observation that can be made with confidence is that Swedish alcohol policy has been innovative. The history of Swedish alcohol control systems can conveniently be divided into four distinct periods. Table 1 shows these periods and makes a few observations about the differences between them. The so-called Gothenburg system was introduced in the mid-nineteenth century and the so-called Bratt system was introduced locally before (and nationally during) the First World War. Both these systems received wide international publicity and apparently influenced alcohol control thinking in other parts of the world. After the abolition of the Bratt system in 1954 there was a period of antagonism towards control in Sweden until the middle of the 1970s when it was replaced by a new wave in favour of control.

Of course, important reforms also took place within each of these periods. Some important events in the history of Swedish alcohol control are summarized in Table 2. It is impossible to understand the evolution of the Swedish system without considering general economic development and changes in methods of alcohol production. Furthermore, the mass mobilization by the temperance movement must be remembered, as must its connection with religious movements, working-class movements and the struggle for democratization, especially through electoral reform.

The Gothenburg system

There had already been a number of attempts to give the state a monopoly of production for fiscal reasons before the introduction of the Gothenburg system. Although it was not until 1855 that a law was introduced placing serious restrictions on the home production of *brännvin* (vodka), changes in production methods had already made vodka cheaper and the law only strengthened a process that was already under way. Another important change was the liberalization of trade laws, opening the market for new types of product. This was one of the factors behind the popular movement for stricter control. In some parts of the country, parishes decided to control the availability of alcoholic drinks. Different parishes adopted different procedures: in some cases there was near prohibition, in others sales limitations. Whatever approach was adopted, local control commanded strong public support.

114

Table 1. The four main alcohol control systems

Period	Name of system	Main emphasis	Main responsible authorities	Basic definition
1850–1915	Gothenburg	Control of economic interest in alcohol	Municipal authorities	Moral question
1916–1954	Bratt	Control of individual drinking	State administration, Royal Control Board	Social question
1955–1975	State monopoly	Freedom and responsibility	State monopoly (weak)	Alcoholism, medical and social question
1976–	State monopoly	New control orientation	State monopoly (weak)	Public health question

Table 2. Important events in the formation
of Swedish alcohol policy

Year	Event
1850	Establishment of Gothenburg system in Falun
1855	Home distilling more or less abolished
1864	Liberty to pursue trade
1913	Profit from alcohol sales to the state
1915	Introduction of individual control in the whole country (the Bratt system)
1917	New alcohol law — extensive restrictions
1922	Referendum with 49% of votes in favour of prohibition
1937	Municipal veto abolished
1955	Bratt system abolished
1965	Introduction of medium beer
1977	Medium beer withdrawn
1978	Advertising ban

One form of control became especially important. The so-called Gothenburg system was first introduced in 1850 in the community of Falun and in 1865 it was adopted by Gothenburg, the second largest city in Sweden. New legislation made it possible for a city or rural commune to give monopoly powers to a company (*bolag*) to distribute alcoholic drinks. This system spread through the country. In some cities *bolaget* only affected restaurants, in others only shops and in some, both. The degree of monopoly differed from city to city and the variation is thought to have depended on the relative strengths of municipal economic interests in alcohol on the one hand and the influence of temperance policy considerations on the other.

Be that as it may, it is clear that one of the major issues discussed by Swedish municipal authorities towards the end of the nineteenth century was alcohol policy. The basic issue was whether profits from the alcohol trade should be reduced in the name of temperance. It seems clear that the underlying goal of the Gothenburg system — to eliminate private economic interest from the alcohol trade — was only partly achieved. In some cases private profit was replaced by municipal economic interests. The history of the Gothenburg system and its impact on the alcohol situation has not yet been written, but it is clear that there was considerable regional variation. The extensive discussions to which the Gothenburg system gave rise created an understanding of alcohol policy issues, with the result that many later control measures must be seen in the perspective of experience with the Gothenburg system.

In fact the economic interest of the municipalities in the alcohol trade became so great that from 1913 onwards the state began to collect the revenue instead. The municipalities did get compensation, however, in the form of state support for other activities. Control became stricter during this period, partly because of the shortage of raw materials during the First World War. In addition, the cities of Gothenburg and Stockholm introduced various controls directed at the individual. One form of control was accepted by the central administration, and later sanctioned by parliament, and is now known as the Bratt system.

The Bratt system

Ivan Bratt was a physician whose writings about the alcohol question between 1909 and 1922 had a remarkable influence in Sweden. His system was supported by the Swedish Medical Association and was seen as an alternative to prohibition. The Swedes rejected prohibition in a referendum in 1922 by a very small margin. In fact Bratt not only outlined an alcohol control system, he developed a "treatment" (control) system based on the view that only a very small proportion of those who abuse alcohol are sick. In fact, he tried to combine these various elements into a comprehensive system.

Without entering into details, the cornerstones of the Bratt system may be described as follows.

1.   The economic interest of the alcohol trade should be controlled by the state.

2.   The distribution of alcoholic drinks should be through municipally controlled shops and restaurants only. For permission to buy from shops, an individual purchase permit would be required; every purchase would be signed by the buyer and registered.

3.   Abuse of alcohol might lead to the withdrawal of the permit.

4.   Abuse of alcohol should be reported to local temperance boards that would have the power to take various measures against abuse.

5.   For cases of extreme forms of abuse a compulsory treatment system should be developed.

Although many of Bratt's ideas were put into practice, the system adopted deviated somewhat from his line of thought. Bratt was successful in eliminating private liquor enterprises and in introducing purchase permits and temperance boards. A maximum limit for purchases was introduced against his advice, however, and the restaurant trade was controlled in a detailed way that would probably have been unacceptable to him.

The Bratt system changed a great deal during its 40 years of existence. It became very centralized through the emergence of a very powerful state administrative organ called the Royal Board of Control, that tried to harmonize a system that had much local variation in its infancy.

Recent developments

The Bratt system was finally abolished following the proposals of a state committee set up in 1944. The forces within the committee who were trying to abolish restrictions were supported by the temperance movement, which had always been critical of Bratt partly because of his victory over the prohibition movement. Abolition of the Bratt system was also supported by those who saw alcohol abuse primarily as a disease.

The Bratt system was abolished with the slogan "Liberty and responsibility", which was intended to introduce a liberal era. The negative effects of the abolition soon made themselves felt, however, forming an obstacle to further liberal reform. Thus, from the middle of the 1970s there emerged signs of a new era of control. A new mass movement arguing for alcohol rationing was formed which could, in many ways, be seen as some sort of return to the Bratt system. Interestingly enough, this movement is dominated by medical doctors, whereas important groups within the temperance movement are hostile to it.

One of the steps taken during this new era of control was the abolition of the so-called medium beer (3.6% alcohol) in 1977. Sweden also has very low alcohol consumption in restaurants. Control of tax deductions for business purposes was introduced in the 1960s, and in the 1970s additional restrictions on alcohol for purposes of state representation were introduced. A ban on alcohol advertising was enforced in 1978.

The United Kingdom: a comparison

Since the place held by alcohol control in the Swedish sociocultural setting is unique to that country, let us take the United Kingdom as an example of a very different approach. Without going into the previous history of alcohol control in that country, it is clear that alcohol policy in the United Kingdom has been a very controversial issue since the early 1970s. It began with the Report of the 1972 Erroll Committee (6) which was in favour of far-reaching liberalization of the liquor licensing laws. Medical and social scientists questioned the scientific basis for the conclusions of the Committee, and over the next five years various documents were produced, for instance by the Royal College of Psychiatrists (7) arguing against the Erroll Committee on behalf of stricter control. This view eventually prevailed and following a report by the Central Policy Review Staff (8) it was finally translated into concrete policy measures.

This attempt by the United Kingdom to develop a national policy is an important lesson for other countries. A large number of government departments (16 in the case of the United Kingdom) may be affected by a change in policy. Those who believe that a national policy can be developed in harmony must realize that there will be areas of conflicting interests. It is beyond the scope of this section to assess how these conflicts were weighed against each other in the policy measures proposed by the British government. It is clear, however, that the government chose to avoid the conflict by adopting an entirely different basis for handling alcohol problems. The model they adopted is sometimes called the "bimodal model", indicating its adherence to the view that there are two distinct populations, one composed of sensible users of alcohol and the other of abusers. Of course, policy may indeed be developed on this basis, as was widely done during the 1950s and 1960s, but it should be pointed out that the bimodal model of alcohol problems has lost much of its scientific credibility.

Conclusions

Policy formation clearly consists of a great deal more than discussions of scientific facts, and the British example gives us an excellent illustration of the obstacles that may arise to impede the development of a national alcohol policy. These obstacles are quite real and it is clear that it is no solution to neglect them. They have to be analysed to create the conditions for further dialogue.

This presentation of the Swedish case and the brief reference to the British case indicate that it is not just a slogan to say that historical and cultural variations must be observed when national alcohol policies are developed. Nevertheless, although policies cannot simply be carried over from one country to another, knowledge gathered in one country does have relevance for others trying to develop national policies.

References

1. **Lenke, L.** Totalkonsumtionens betydelse för alkoholskadeutvecklingen i Sverige [The impact of overall alcohol consumption on the development of alcohol damage in Sweden]. *Sociologisk forskning,* **20**: 45–47 (1983).
2. **Frånberg, P.** Umeåsystemet. En studie i alternativ nykterhetspolitik 1915–1945 [The Umeå system. Study of an alternative temperance policy 1915–1945]. *In: Umeå studies in the humanities, Vol. 50.* Umeå, Acta Universitatis Umensis, 1983.
3. **Thulin, I. & Marcus, M.** *Göteborgssystemet 1865–1945* [The Gothenburg system 1865–1945]. Gothenburg, 1947.
4. **Lundkvist, S.** Politik, nykterhet och reformer. En studie i folkrörelsernas politiska verksamhet 1900–1920 [Policy, temperance and reform. A study on the popular movement's political actions 1900–1920]. *Studia historica upsaliensia 53.* Uppsala, 1974.
5. **Åberg, I.** Folkrörelsernas politiska aktivitet i Gävle under 1880-talet [The political activities of the popular movement in Gälve in the 1880s]. *Studia historica upsaliensia 68.* Uppsala, 1975.
6. **Home Office.** *Report of the Departmental Committee on Liquor Licensing.* London, H.M. Stationery Office, 1972.
7. **Royal College of Psychiatrists.** *Alcohol and alcoholism:* report of a special committee on alcohol and alcoholism. London, Tavistock, 1979.
8. **Central Policy Review Staff.** *Alcohol policies in the United Kingdom.* Stockholm, Sociologiska Institutionen, 1982.

7

International aspects of the prevention of alcohol problems: research experiences and perspectives

P. Sulkunen

Of all the misconceptions about the role of science in policy-making, probably the most serious is the fallacy that research can from its own resources find ready solutions to all the world's problems. It is false to think that the only thing left once a social problem has been recognized is to call in researchers to find ways of getting rid of it. Such fallacies, not uncommon among the scientific community itself in the postwar years of optimism and progress, lead to unreasonable expectations that turn into frustration and despair when the limits of political and economic reality become apparent.

What science *can* do is to support reasonable policy-makers in their efforts to articulate the nature of problems, to define their dimensions and to locate accessible points where corrective action can be applied. The alcohol problem, like other social problems, cannot be solved simply by the efforts of science and rationality. It changes its nature; it varies from one society to the next and from one historical period to another. At its most helpful, research can bring to light what in each historical context is the core of the question and call attention to its most aggravating aspects at that time and place.

Economics and Politics versus Public Health

If one single major conclusion from the research on alcohol problems over the last ten years were to be identified as having special relevance to the international aspects of alcohol control, it would be this: economic and political interests, and often ideological assumptions as well, have been largely in conflict with public health interests in the postwar period, especially in North America and western Europe. This conflict has been particularly aggravated where traditional consumption patterns have changed — which in most cases has meant an increase in the overall consumption of alcohol — and where the market for alcoholic drinks has consequently been restructured. At the same time, economic and political conditions have increased the opportunities for the interplay of market forces, whereas the scope for public health action has been essentially reduced.

From the public health point of view, the major concern in the postwar period has been the persistent and marked increase in alcohol consumption. In some of the western countries that saw the greatest boom of prosperity, consumption doubled or tripled in a relatively short time.

In the western industrialized societies there was nothing and nobody to defend the public health arguments. Consumers, in general, had no sympathy for controls, especially for systems of control that dated back to the prewar period. The market for consumer goods was rapidly expanding into new commodities and the exotic world of alcoholic drinks offered some of the most lucrative opportunities for capital investment. Control of any sort was not seen as being in the industry's interest either, at least not so long as there was room for expansion and for newcomers.

Today, the reaction to the issue of controls is as follows: we want to know more; we want to predict the consequences for health of particular consumption levels; we want to assure ourselves and others of the effectiveness of control policies in order to argue for regulation and against vested interests; we want to calculate the costs of alcohol problems to society in order to argue for controls on the same grounds as those who argue against them; and we want more reassurance that controls work.

The Need for more Research

In contrast to ten years ago, a call for more research is no longer the answer. Instead the time has come for a serious reflection on the meaning of the major conclusions of existing research. An examination of these conclusions from a policy perspective may help determine what and how much further research is needed before any rational action can be taken.

This is important, since the more usual process of compiling lists of research topics, before any policy measures are even considered, can very easily become simply an attempt to camouflage passivity. In view of the conflict between the public health point of view and other considerations concerning the availability of alcohol, such passivity may be understandable, but it is not necessarily reasonable. The interests opposing a public health orientation in alcohol policy are not necessarily flawlessly monolithic, even at the international level. Especially in an era when the market is stable, or even contracting, market regulation may become an important issue from perspectives other than that of public health. The greatest challenge to political wisdom is to find strategic allies in a battlefield that is full of conflicting interest groups.

If the world can discuss disarmament, health for all and the abolition of hunger, it is hard to see why it cannot be brought to discuss alcohol control. Of course, the condition for such discussions is that the objections of those whose financial interests are at stake are taken seriously. There is no point in isolating public health concerns into a defensive position. It is time for action, but it should be recognized that action cannot be taken heedless of the obstacles.

122

Consumption level and public health

One of the most important concerns of alcohol research over the last ten years has been the relationship between the overall consumption of alcohol and the rates of alcohol-related health problems. This discussion, originally opened by Ledermann in France and later developed by the researchers at the Addiction Research Foundation of Ontario, Canada, has been summarized in the collaborative work, produced under the auspices of the WHO Regional Office for Europe, entitled *Alcohol control policies in public health perspective (1)*. This book explains the theoretical and empirical reasons why alcohol-related health problems can be expected to vary with the level of overall consumption. It also documents the fact that in the postwar period, and especially since the 1960s, alcohol consumption has increased in most of the countries for which adequate data are available.

Since then, concern about the public health implications of increasing alcohol consumption has found its way into numerous international documents and in some countries it has been adopted as the guiding principle of government policies on alcohol issues *(2,3)*. At the Conference on Public Health Aspects of Alcohol and Drug Dependence, organized by the WHO Regional Office for Europe in Dubrovnik in 1978, this principle was discussed extensively and in detail. The report of the Conference noted rising consumption trends and then stated: "The view was generally accepted that there was an association between increasing *per capita* consumption of alcohol and growth in related problems" *(4)*. In terms of policy-making, this is similar to the position adopted in *Alcohol control policies in public health perspective,* which is that since alcohol consumption affects the health of the people and control measures can limit this consumption, then control of the availability of alcohol becomes a public health issue.

This conclusion and its theoretical and empirical justifications have not been left undisputed. Some of the counter-arguments have been launched by interested parties with pragmatic goals, while others have taken the form of more serious scientific efforts to find counter-evidence or to locate weak points in the basis for the conclusions. Yet others have been discontented with the limitation of the argument to the relation between alcohol and consequences for health, when it is known that alcohol creates a wide variety of problems that cannot legitimately be classified as health problems. Equally, it has been noted that many alcohol-related problems depend on the circumstances in which alcohol is used as well as on the quantities consumed. What is interesting in the debate is not so much the face value of the sophisticated, often statistical arguments, but the context of the debate itself.

The interest of alcohol researchers in this area was a reaction to the growth in consumption, to the relaxation of traditional control measures and to the superficial sociological defences of the liberalist alcohol policies that prevailed in the late 1970s *(5)*. This reaction grew from national experiences at that time when it was not known how widespread the growing consumption was or how serious its possible consequences actually were for the world. The least that can be said about the impact of research in this area is that it alerted policy-makers to the fact that there is a price to pay for unfettered growth. Judging from the reception of *Alcohol control policies in public health perspective* among policy-makers, both at national and international levels, the message was, if not accepted, at least clearly noted.

From the policy-making point of view, the notion that a growth in consumption carries public health risks is of course an uncomfortable one, particularly when, to so many branches of industry and trade, alcoholic drinks are a source of productivity and profit. It would, of course, be presumptuous to expect that the public health argument alone would be sufficient to move governments and international organizations to change their course of action. This is another reason to study the mechanisms that have given rise to such a growth in consumption in the past and to understand the laxity of government reactions to it. Economic interests have always been there, so the essential question is why on the one hand they are so important and powerful in this particular period, while on the other hand all the social forces seem to have gone that could support more careful control of the industry. The idea of control is not in itself new; what is new about the postwar period is that these systems have been left to deteriorate and their original justifications have been ignored.

Research into these issues has been undertaken in several research centres independently, but a major effort to record national experiences and make comparisons between them was organized, again in collaboration with the WHO European Regional Office, into the international study of alcohol control experiences *(5,6)*, a comparative study of the social history of alcohol control in seven countries. In and around this study, quite extensive research was undertaken that can be useful in estimating the major factors in alcohol policy today.

Effects of European economic integration
Since the phenomenon of growing consumption and changing patterns of alcohol use has been an international one, it is natural to look for its roots in international mechanisms affecting industry and trade. It is possible that this phenomenon is an unintended side effect of more general international industrial and commercial developments that occurred at the same time. In Europe, the first inquiry must be into the role of international economic integration, given that the countries of western Europe originally had very different production and consumption traditions that now seem to be mixing and blending. What is the role of increasing trade among the European Community countries and what particular mechanisms are altering their alcohol economies?

Measuring the causal effects of integration on consumption is no less problematic than measuring the causal effects on consumption of any single social factor. From a policy point of view, what is most important is to identify the areas of European Community activity that do deal with alcohol and that have an impact on the conditions in which it is made available in the member states, as well as on the conditions within which the member states can exercise control in their pursuit of public health goals.

The freeing of trade

Since the establishment of the European Economic Community (EEC) by the Treaty of Rome, its impact on alcohol availability has been felt in four major ways (7). The first EEC programme was the abolition of customs tariffs and export/import quotas from trade between member countries. For the original six member countries, this process was completed by the end of the 1960s, although the free trade principle was extended in a modified form in the Yaoundé and Lomé conventions to include the former colonies of the member states. The general principle of free trade already had some importance as regards the possibility of controlling alcohol availability at a national level. For example, the monopolies of France and the Federal Republic of Germany have had to comply with a number of EEC rulings on quotas and tariffs by reducing traditional control measures that have been seen by the Commission as discriminatory.

The general liberation of trade from such obstacles has facilitated the increase of trade in alcoholic drinks within the Community and limited the capacity of national governments to exercise alcohol control. It can be maintained that free trade as such is not an inducement to increased alcohol use, as its only purpose and function is to set competing products on equal terms in national and international markets. It is undeniable, however, that where the introduction of new types of drink is an essential element in the growth of overall consumption, free trade is one of the factors that contribute to this growth, or at least do not hinder it.

The Common Wine Policy

Alcoholic drinks are not ordinary commodities within the European Community. They are largely of agricultural origin, and wine is officially classified as an agricultural product. Thus the second EEC programme that had an impact on the alcoholic drinks market was the gradual adoption of the Common Agricultural Policy in the 1960s and its application through the Common Wine Policy that has been in operation since 1970. The EEC policy on alcoholic drinks, in the context of the abolition of tariffs and quotas, consisted simply of passive application of general Community rules. In the case of the Common Wine Policy, however, the Community undertook an active and well articulated long-term programme specifically with respect to one alcoholic drink. The goals of the programme paid no attention to the fact that the alcohol contained in this drink is potentially harmful to health. The Common Wine Policy consists of: a system of price control and intervention procedures; a common organization of trade in wine with countries outside the Community; rules for the production and planting of vines and rules concerning some oenological practices; and the classification of wines and viticultural areas within the Community (8). The aims of this Policy are those of the Common Agricultural Policy: to secure a tolerable and stable income for the farming sector through stable price levels; to achieve a stable balance of supply and demand within the Community; to regulate trade with countries outside the Community in a coordinated manner; to promote structural reform within agriculture for greater productivity and rationalization; and to ensure equitable supplies to consumers (9,10).

The most important effect of the implementation of the Common Wine Policy has been an essential diversion of trade in wine from extra-Community imports to intra-Community trade. Furthermore, the price level has been effectively kept stable or has risen and the average quality of the wine has improved. On the other hand, the system has not been able to reduce oversupply, partly because it has provided a guaranteed price level and partly because it has supported technological improvements leading to greater productivity *(7,11)*.

The Alcohol Regime

The third programme of the EEC related to alcoholic drinks was the Alcohol Regime. The abolition of quotas and tariffs by no means completed progress towards the free movement of goods within the Community. Ethyl alcohol is in this respect a particularly interesting commodity. First, its production is an important outlet for agricultural oversupplies and thus the quantity of alcohol for sale in the Community does not depend only on free market forces; second, ethyl alcohol is a chemical that takes many forms in many industries; and third, it can be produced by very different methods and from many different raw materials at widely varying costs. For these reasons, almost all countries have developed a system of regulating the alcohol market in order to provide cheap alcohol for industrial purposes while reserving the more expensive types of alcohol for use in the cosmetic industries and for drinks. Furthermore, alcohol is usually taxed according to its intended use. These systems create an indispensable need for control to prevent fraud and to stabilize the market. Since 1972 the Commission has made an effort to establish a common system of regulating the market for ethyl alcohol, but for several reasons it has not so far been able to carry it through.

Tax harmonization

The fourth EEC programme that has been directly linked to alcohol availability is tax harmonization. The Treaty of Rome stipulates, in rather vague terms, that indirect taxes in the Community shall be harmonized (Articles 99 and 100). Furthermore, it lays down in Article 95 that:

> no Member State shall impose, directly or indirectly on the products of other Member States any internal taxation of any kind in excess of that imposed directly or indirectly on similar domestic products. Furthermore, no Member State shall impose on products of other Member States any internal taxation of such a nature as to afford indirect protection to other products.

Indeed, the Community has been able to harmonize general indirect taxation to a considerable extent in the form of Value Added Tax (VAT). The second major form of indirect taxation, namely excise duties, directly concerns alcoholic drinks. The existence of very different systems and levels of excise duties between member states has created the need to maintain border controls to prevent profiteering by transporting goods from countries where they are only taxed at a low level to countries where the excise

126

levied on them is high. In 1972 the Council decided that excise duties should be harmonized in two phases: first the structures and then the levels.

In fact there has been very little progress in this area. Pending appropriate Community legislation, the Commission has proceeded in exactly the opposite order to that prescribed in the 1972 Resolution and has resorted to the European Court of Justice to eradicate tax differences between domestic and imported spirits in Denmark, France and Italy. The Commission has also acted against the United Kingdom's practice of levying very different tax rates on beer and on wine. This case depends on whether beer and wine are in fact similar products and the legal debate over this question has produced some curious arguments about the sociological and economic definitions of these drinks. Since, however, the Court and the Commission agree that alcohol is the essence of them both, the average alcohol content will be the decisive guideline in establishing the legally acceptable relationship between beer and wine tax levels (12).

The effects of European integration
Thus the four major areas of Community activities that have had a direct bearing on the availability of alcohol have been the general opening of frontiers to trade, the Common Wine Policy, and the efforts to establish both the Alcohol Regime and tax harmonization. There is a fifth programme concerned with impediments to trade other than fiscal and economic ones, namely issues such as technical requirements, package size and advertising regulations, but discussion of them here is precluded by limits of space.

A recent study on the effects of economic integration on the availability of alcohol (7) led to the following conclusions.

1. The general elimination of tariffs and quotas has stimulated exports from some Community countries to others where the level of consumption of a particular type of drink has been low. Free trade increases international competition and in some cases leads to price reductions.

2. The Common Wine Policy has, in particular, promoted such internal trade. The prices and incomes policy of the Common Wine Policy has taken precedence over structural policy; furthermore, structural policy has been directed towards improving the quality of wine and rationalizing production methods, rather than curbing rising production.

3. Although the market in ethyl alcohol has not yet been organized, continuing discussions suggest that, when established, the Alcohol Regime will be unlikely to aim at reducing the production of alcohol for the drinks trade. Instead, it may contribute to rationalization and eliminate the remaining impediments to trade in distilled alcoholic drinks. The most obvious trade restrictions that violated the Treaty of Rome have already been eliminated, even without the help of a common alcohol regime.

4.   Excise harmonization has proceeded slowly, but this programme is also being continually discussed in the Community. When these discussions lead to legal arguments, it is likely that excise duties will have to be lowered in countries where they are exceptionally high (Denmark, Ireland and the United Kingdom).

Some more recent studies lend support to these conclusions. Kortteinen *(11)* has, for instance, shown that the Common Wine Policy has failed to drain the wine lake. Indeed, it can be argued that the various strategies to promote structural change have actually led to a worsening of the problem, since the reduction of viticultural land has been more than compensated for by the rise in productivity that has resulted from replanting and capital investments. Equally, the example of tax harmonization in the United Kingdom suggests that it will almost certainly lead to a lowering of the overall level of alcohol taxation and to a consequent rise in consumption *(12)*.

Conclusions

The role of the EEC is not limited to harmonizing taxes, duties, rules of competition or industrial and agricultural policies, but extends to the harmonization of consumption patterns. In the particular area of alcohol consumption, it has an inbuilt tendency to harmonize consumption upwards. Although many of the Community programmes and policies have already contributed to this effect, it must be emphasized that the system of free trade is still largely incomplete as regards alcoholic drinks. Discussions on the remaining problems continue and, if successful, their results are very likely to reinforce this tendency towards less rigorous control and towards harmonization of national control policies and of consumption patterns. The main conclusion to be drawn from the historical experience of integration in western Europe is perhaps that the structures of the EEC do not encourage public health concern in any major form. The Commission sees its mandate as purely economic and tends to take a legalistic view in its policy judgements. The Council of Ministers concentrates on negotiating the balance of costs and benefits of the EEC policies to each nation, while the European Parliament, which is the body that potentially might be the advocate of broader health and welfare concerns, is relatively powerless and lacks the technical means of proposing alternatives.

Activities undertaken by the Commission in connection wtih the public health implications of its economic policies on alcoholic drinks have been very limited. In 1977 the Health and Safety Directorate of the Commission, in collaboration with WHO and the International Council on Alcohol and Addictions, invited a group of experts to discuss the problem. The group stated in its conclusions that:

> the Community should not regard alcoholic beverages as simply another food or drink, because of its toxic effects. As a matter of urgency the CEC [Commission of the European Communities] should review its current economic practices in order to minimize the hazard from alcohol to health and social wellbeing. In

particular, the Community and individual Member States need to consider their policies on alcohol production and its promotion, with a view to reducing its consumption.[a]

This is simply the conclusion of the group, however, not of the Commission, and a subsequent meeting of experts called by the Health and Safety Directorate in 1983 seems to have been the only practical consequence of the earlier meeting.

Given this situation, important initiatives are perhaps most likely to emerge at national and local level. But activities at that level are weak and remain ineffective without the technical advice and expertise available at international level. The processes that have a bearing on the availability of alcohol in the Community are continuous and cannot be separated from day-to-day decision-making. From a public health perspective, what is most needed is the capacity to follow and scrutinize the EEC policies regularly in order to arouse public discussion, to disseminate information and to search for alternative approaches. Only in very specific cases does the impact of integration in western Europe require large-scale individual research. A standing committee of investigation vested with some authority could, for instance, provide an effective counterbalance to the lack of health and welfare concerns in the EEC structures.

Tourism and alcohol

Tourism is another factor that is often given as a possible explanation of the tendency towards homogenization of drinking patterns and consumption levels. The number of tourists visiting other countries, including some parts of the developing world, has grown immensely since the early 1960s. Between 1964 and 1979 the number of international tourist arrivals at frontiers increased from 100 million to almost 600 million. There is, however, surprisingly little research on this question in comparison to the frequency of allusions made to its importance. It may be that the importance of tourism is not so much in the magnitude of its effects as in its strategic nature. The diffusion and internationalization of consumption styles is something that results almost inevitably not only from tourism but from all other types of cultural contact, which in themselves are positive enrichments of people's lives.

There is, however, one special reason why tourism may cause concern from the public health point of view. Duty-free sales of alcohol as well as of tobacco and some luxury items are often used as a lure to tourists as well as a means of subsidizing certain transport industries. Mosher & Ralston[b] have shown that the use of duty-free alcohol as a lure to tourists in the Caribbean

---

[a] *The medico-social risks of alcohol consumption* (report of a working party prepared for the Commission of the European Communities, 1979).

[b] **Mosher, J.F. & Ralston, L.D.** *Tourism, alcohol problems and the international trade in alcoholic beverages.* A case study of two Caribbean Islands and the impact of US tax policy (paper presented at the First Meeting of the International Group for Comparative Alcohol Studies, Switzerland, October 1982).

region not only affects the consumption of the visitors but also has a widespread influence on the availability of alcohol and on drinking problems among the host population. The recent practice of giving alcohol entirely free to some passengers in aeroplanes is another example of the use of alcohol as a lure. Regardless of how effective such methods may be as a lure, there is no logical justification for offering the travelling public a more advantageous opportunity to buy alcohol than those who rarely or never travel. A direct risk, particularly to those who travel a great deal and are thus exposed to an unnecessarily great amount of alcohol, is that they are encouraged to consume more than they otherwise would.

Although perhaps not the most serious concern of public health, the sale of duty-free alcohol is symbolically important. Exemption from duties was once a way of securing for travellers a reasonable and just right to import rare articles for their own use, as souvenirs or as gifts. Today, duty-free sales of alcohol, tobacco and perfumes are a multimillion dollar business that is rapidly expanding. Although duty-free sales, which consist mostly of alcohol (40%) and tobacco (30%), have grown into an essential part of the tourist industry their rationale is hard to understand, especially since this advantage is not given to all international travellers. In Europe, only those who travel by boat or by air enjoy the advantages of duty-free shops. The original justification was that once a boat or an air carrier is on international waters or in international airspace, it is open to dispute who is entitled to collect the duties. This justification no longer holds since, in the European Community for example, all the duty-free shops in airports are within the customs union, and furthermore only a marginal amount of duty-free business is actually carried out in the air. Whereas originally the exemptions were from duties, they now concern both excise levies and the normal VAT. The reasons for the existence of this publicly accepted tax avoidance are, of course, economic since private enterprises make exceptionally high profits at the expense of the state. While it is true that a large part of the high mark-ups in duty-free shops is reimbursed to airport authorities or used to cover the operating costs of passenger boats, it is worth remembering that up to three quarters of these revenues come from articles involving health risks. If part of the consumption thus provoked would not take place without the added incentive of the low price, it is important to ask whether it is necessary to pay for the operation of airports or passenger boats by increasing the risk to public health.

Alcohol and tourism is an area where no government can act alone, but there is as yet no international forum for discussing these problems from a comprehensive perspective, taking into account ethical and social concerns as well as commercial and fiscal considerations. This is an area where research could assist, but the essential problem is to transcend the boundaries between the economic, fiscal and public health branches of international organizations. A very small research input could clarify the questions, identify the dimensions of the problem and locate the various interests involved; but research alone is fruitless without some willingness to act on the part of international bodies. Of course, any advance of public health arguments in actual policy-making will arouse objections from interested

130

parties, but that is no reason why the representatives of the public health point of view should not voice their criticisms.

Growth in the production of alcohol

One of the most important conclusions of researchers in the 1970s was that any national effort to promote the public health point of view in alcohol control must tackle the underlying economic interests involved.

The alcoholic drinks industries in all parts of the world rapidly became modernized after the Second World War. In the early 1960s, alcoholic drinks were still largely agricultural products, manufactured on a small scale with most of the production going to local use. Production for international markets was important only in a few special cases, and even today internationally distributed alcohol accounts for only a small part of total world production. Thus, alcoholic drinks were very much like other basically agricultural foodstuffs, which have only slowly and unevenly become more widely commercialized (13).

The industrialization of alcohol production has been accompanied by an enormous increase in production capacity. It is estimated that the minimum efficient production capacity of a brewing plant has grown from about one million barrels a year in 1960 to roughly four million in 1978. In viticulture the yields per hectare are constantly increasing, while in distilling the progress is even more dramatic. In very many cases, production capacity expanded in the boom years after the Second World War, in the expectation that the growth in consumption would continue. In more recent years, as consumption trends have levelled off, a structural overcapacity has resulted, not only in viticulture but in the alcoholic drinks industries as a whole.

Conglomerates and multinationals

This growth in production capacity has been made possible by concentrated capital investment. This concentration was necessary, not only to mobilize resources for industrial investments, but also to restructure the marketing networks to correspond to large-scale production. Conglomeration is another important factor in this process (14). Alcohol industries no longer limit their operations to the production or distribution of alcoholic drinks but are now intertwined in a complex industrial and commercial system of ownership and control relationships between apparently independent companies. What is even more important from the point of view of international alcohol control is that this system is largely multinational. When a conglomerate that is internationally owned operates in several branches of the production and distribution of consumer goods, it has both the interest and the power to influence national control legislation. In this way it can harmonize its own marketing strategies and facilitate its products' access to potential new consumer groups.

The interest of such conglomerates in new groups of drinkers and in new marketing areas has become even greater in the 1970s and early 1980s as consumption growth has slowed down in the industrialized countries. Cavanagh (14) found that the alcoholic drinks industries have started extensive operations in developing countries and in other areas where alcohol

131

consumption has so far been low. He estimates that the developing countries have contributed disproportionately to the growth of global imports of alcoholic drinks: for example, 42 of the 46 countries in the world where beer consumption increased by more than 50% between 1975 and 1980 are classified as developing countries. The expansion of the alcoholic drinks markets in developing countries is not limited to imports of drinks from industrialized countries. The alcoholic drinks conglomerates also mobilize extensive exports of technology and capital to be invested in the alcohol industries of these countries, thus leading to further increases in global capacity for alcohol production.

It is clear that alcoholic drinks control is no longer possible at an exclusively national level. The production and distribution systems have now become so internationalized that any country that wishes to protect its population against unwanted inflows of alcoholic drinks needs some form of international collaboration. Equally, since new markets are especially attractive to the industries, there is a risk of sudden exposure to large quantities of alcohol in countries that have little experience of its use, a risk that is all the more alarming because these countries often have more than enough problems of health and nutrition without the added burden of drinking problems.

In the discussion on economic integration and duty-free alcohol, it was suggested that research already provided some clear results with implications for international alcohol control. By contrast, in relation to the issue of global production and trade and the economic problems involved, it is increasingly obvious that our ignorance remains enormous and our understanding is far from sufficient even to suggest a policy approach. Developments in the global production of and trade in alcoholic drinks may arouse moral concerns but morality in itself is not practical policy. It needs to be supplemented with a more thorough understanding of the economic factors behind the tendency towards an increasing supply of alcohol in the world.

Where research is needed
Alcohol production and distribution have become part of the wider complex of agricultural, industrial and political interests. There seems to be a tendency to maintain agricultural overproduction in industrialized countries, while hampering the rational development of food production in developing countries. Furthermore, industrialized countries tend to transform an unnecessarily large part of this overproduction into alcohol. These tendencies are supported not only by the industries themselves but also by national and international agricultural policies, such as the Common Wine Policy of the EEC. Extensive research into the global alcohol economy is still required, to achieve a better understanding of the mechanisms that maintain extensive and expanding alcohol production when the opposite is what is needed.

This is an area where the role of research is essential and this should be reflected in international alcohol programmes. Two types of study could be envisaged. First, in countries where extensive production increases are being planned, case studies could be useful in showing what mechanisms are at work to create this need in the first place, and also in determining what

132

precautions could be taken to circumvent any possible adverse consequences. Second, global collaborative studies are needed to screen the possibilities of preventing the unnecessary transformation of agricultural resources into alcohol in a world that already suffers from extensive malnutrition. In this type of study, the problem is very complex indeed, since it involves a thorough knowledge of alcohol production structures and of the agro-industrial complex as a whole, in a range of different social and economic circumstances.

Data

Experience in other areas of comprehensive health policies shows that one of the first steps towards success is to establish a satisfactory data monitoring system. This is because developments in the dimensions of the problem require continuous, and preferably historical, screening of core indicators. The construction of a data monitoring system can serve educational and administrative purposes as well as providing an essential basis for continuing research.

This is especially true at an international level, since the development of an international alcohol control policy requires accurate, reliable and up-to-date data on the production, trade and consumption of alcoholic drinks. The importance of such data has been underlined in the official statements of various WHO bodies and working groups, including the World Health Assembly resolutions WHA28.81 in 1975 and WHA32.40 in 1979 and the Expert Committee on Problems Related to Alcohol Consumption (3). Researchers have to use available data on consumption, production and trade as well as on the adverse consequences of alcohol use, whenever they attempt to respond to calls for comparative research from both international organizations and individual governments.

Yet these data remain today the responsibility either of private or of national research institutions. It is difficult not to see a contradiction between the repeated invitations to researchers to contribute to policy discussions on the one hand and, on the other, the reluctance of international organizations to play their part in providing the most essential and basic tools that the researchers need to prepare such contributions. The work is neither very difficult nor costly in comparison with many other international preventive activities. In itself it would be a recognition by the administrators of the long-accepted principle that the availability of alcohol and the economic factors underlying it are of direct concern to the promotion of public health in the alcohol field. International data are kept on the mass media, on crime, on mortality and on morbidity. This shows that the importance of historical trends and international comparisons in these areas is recognized, although the technical difficulties in some of them are greater than in the case of alcoholic drinks. Only the involvement of international organizations can lead to the level of international coordination necessary to find solutions.

The resolutions of the World Health Assembly and the acceptance of the principle that the availability of alcohol is a public health issue are unambiguous in their recognition of the need for such data. It is more difficult, however, to determine to what extent and how WHO should take responsibility for the actual work in meeting this need. Given the relevance of these data to public health interests and to alcohol researchers, WHO evidently does have an important role to play. It is clear, nevertheless, that data on alcohol consumption, production and trade deviate in nature from data on health, morbidity and mortality. Furthermore, the sources of these data are usually to be found in economic rather than medical institutions. Thus, it may be more advisable for these technical reasons for the actual statistical work to be left to a specialized institution, but the importance of a WHO initiative becomes vital in order to guarantee the continuing potency of the public health perspective.

Conclusions

The position advanced in this chapter is that the role of international organizations should not be limited to organizing research but should be extended whenever feasible to implementing the results of that research. This is not to deny the role of international expert organizations in convening specialists to reach a consensus on important scientific issues. Sometimes such a consensus may itself influence national policy-makers.

As regards the international aspects of the prevention of alcohol problems, such an organizational role is not sufficient. Even symbolic interventions into the international decision-making process on alcohol are more efficient as a means of alerting governments, international bodies and indeed the public to the fact that alcohol is a special commodity, the use of which carries a health risk. Only when such intervention is accepted as one of the legitimate roles of international expert organizations, will it be fruitful and reasonable to call for more research into the international aspects of the prevention of alcohol problems.

The obstacles to intervention on questions of availability should be known and recognized in order not to isolate the public health perspective. Consumers' resistance to accepting government control over their consumption habits is perhaps greater now than it was before, while the economic and political interests vested in the alcohol industries are stronger and involve more people than ever. It is probably impossible to return to a situation where the moral and public health concerns about alcohol problems have enough weight to surmount these obstacles on their own, but when public health oriented alcohol control can align itself with other forces working in the same direction, success will be more likely. One example of such an area is duty-free trade, since there are other independent reasons (competition from the tax-paying sector, public revenues and consumer equity) for imposing regulations. Whenever these opportunities arise, the advocates of public health should be ready to intervene and to present their point of view. Another type of situation is where public health oriented alcohol control can be made part of a more general health policy, as in the case of malnutrition in countries where scarce agricultural supplies are at risk of being used increasingly for the production of alcohol.

The major point of this chapter is that the role of alcohol research should no longer be to defend the public health argument in general but to focus on implementation. To do so, its most important functions should be to locate feasible points of intervention, to map out the obstacles, to identify possible social forces working in parallel with the advancement of public health, and to clarify the difficulties involved in developing efficient and realistic programmes of action. The form of public health intervention will vary from case to case. In the case of international trade policies, the ideal approach might be some kind of a standing committee of investigation that would review the day-to-day policies of international bodies and comment on them from the public health perspective. In the case of alcohol and tourism, a better form of intervention might be a round-table consultation where different interest groups and policy-makers could be brought together to discuss their willingness to limit duty-free sales of alcohol and to assess the possibilities of compensation for the inconvenience caused by such limitations. The problem of the overproduction of alcohol for drinking purposes would require a much deeper perspective and here the research input should be substantial.

A precondition for any contribution by researchers is, however, that they be provided with the essential material on which to base their work. There is no single set of material that is more important for research on international aspects of prevention than international data on the production of, trade in and consumption of alcoholic drinks. There is no more appropriate agent for the continuous collection of such data than the international organizations. Even if the practical work should, depending on the circumstances, be carried out by national research institutions, the administrative role of international organizations is absolutely essential.

References

1. **Bruun, K. et al.** *Alcohol control policies in public health perspective.* Forssa, The Finnish Foundation for Alcohol Studies, 1975, Vol. 25.
2. WHO Technical Report Series, No. 551, 1974 (*Twentieth report of the WHO Expert Committee on Drug Dependence*).
3. WHO Technical Report Series, No. 650, 1980 (*Report of the WHO Expert Committee on Problems Related to Alcohol Consumption*).
4. *Public health aspects of alcohol and drug dependence:* report on a WHO Conference. Copenhagen, WHO Regional Office for Europe, 1979 (EURO Reports and Studies, No. 8).
5. **Mäkelä, K. et al.** *Alcohol, society, and the state. Vol. 1: a comparative study of alcohol control.* Toronto, Addiction Research Foundation, 1981.
6. **Single, E. et al., ed.** *Alcohol, society and the state. Vol. 2: the social history of control policy in seven countries.* Toronto, Addiction Research Foundation, 1981.
7. **Sulkunen, P.** *Developments in the availability of alcoholic beverages in the EEC countries.* Helsinki, Social Research Institute of Alcohol Studies, 1978 (Report No. 121).

8. **Commission of the European Communities.** *Les dossiers de la politique agricole commune — le vin,* **49** (1976).

9. **Paxton, J.** *The developing Common Market.* London, Macmillan, 1976.

10. **Bowler, I.R.** The CAP and the space economy of agriculture in the EEC. *In:* Lee, R. & Ogden, P.E., ed. *Economy and society in the EEC.* Saxon House, 1976.

11. **Kortteinen, T.** *Economic integration and the availability of alcoholic beverages in the European Community since 1975.* Helsinki, Social Resarch Institute of Alcohol Studies, 1983 (Reports from the Social Research Institute of Alcohol Studies, No. 30).

12. **Maynard, A. & O'Brien, B.** Harmonisation policies in the European Community and alcohol abuse. *British journal of addiction,* **77**: 235–244 (1982).

13. **Sulkunen, P.** Production, consumption and recent changes of consumption of alcoholic beverages. Part 1. The production and consumption of alcoholic beverages. *British journal of addiction,* **71**: 3–11 (1976).

14. **Cavanagh, J.** The trade debate. *In:* Grant, M. & Ritson, B. *Alcohol, the prevention debate.* London, Croom Helm, 1983.

8

Formulating comprehensive national alcohol policies

K.E. Bruun

In the last ten years, the search for national alcohol policies has gained more and more importance. Although some countries have a long tradition of alcohol policy, it is striking how alcohol control has only recently come to be discussed in broad international meetings. Rather than trying to give a historical account of this, a few points in the chain of events will illustrate the trend. The conclusion from the publication *Alcohol control policies in public health perspective (1)*, makes a suitable starting point since it represents an argument for a health-oriented policy:

> Changes in the overall consumption of alcoholic beverages have a bearing on the health of the people in any society. Alcohol control measures can be used to limit consumption: thus, control of alcohol availability becomes a public health issue.

This conclusion was debated at the WHO Conference on Public Health Aspects of Alcohol and Drug Dependence held in Dubrovnik in 1978 where one of the recommendations urged governments "to develop national strategies in order to prohibit further increases of alcohol consumption or if possible to effect a decrease" *(2)*.

An international review of the prevention of alcohol-related problems observed that 18 Member States of WHO in Europe had national bodies that were expected to handle alcohol problems from a broader perspective than is possible for health authorities *(3)*. The existence of such bodies, however, does not guarantee that national policies have been developed. It is obvious that there is a discrepancy between the wish to develop a national alcohol policy on the one hand and the actual formation of a programme on the other. The need for a policy is therefore expressed in several later WHO documents and meetings. An expert committee that sat in 1980 *(4)*, the Technical Discussions of the World Health Assembly in May 1982[a] and the WHO Board meeting in January 1983, all argue in the same direction. The

---

[a] *Alcohol consumption and alcohol-related problems: development of national policies and programmes* (unpublished WHO document A35/Technical Discussion/1, 1982).

Board gives a clear recommendation "to formulate an explicit and comprehensive national alcohol policy with prevention as a priority".[a] This view is endorsed by the World Health Assembly in its resolution WHA36.12: "recognizing that an effective strategy to tackle the alcohol-related problems necessitates comprehensive national alcohol policies".

We may therefore talk about a real challenge to those responsible for developing national policies. In this chapter an attempt is made to contribute to the discussion about how this challenge can be met. One major problem is to give adequate weight to particular historical and cultural factors while at the same time using international experience and research results. In attempting to relate local matters to generalizations, it is necessary to understand as much as possible about the historical development of alcohol policies in the country in question, before attempting to apply any formula based on existing general knowledge. This chapter, however, concentrates on that second phase, setting out some decisive steps in the formation of a national policy, including basic points of departure such as the data base needed to formulate actual stages in policy development. The possible role of international organizations is also discussed. The aim of the chapter is to establish some very optimistic guidelines that, when applied to a particular country, will make it possible to formulate a national alcohol policy where cultural traits are observed without neglecting knowledge gained from other countries.

Points of Departure

It is important to state the points of departure for any programme as explicitly as possible. This discussion takes for granted, however, that the extensive literature concerning alcohol issues and research already published, especially during the 1970s, forms an adequate background for accepting the basic need to establish an alcohol policy. The statement that there indeed exists a firm foundation for developing the content of a national policy is based on the fact that the conclusions of the publication *Alcohol control policies in public health perspective (1)* have been widely accepted and turned into requests for such policies.

Existing knowledge and policy recommendations cannot be applied to individual countries without explicit consideration of cultural and historical traditions and an understanding of how matters currently stand *(1)*.[b] The examples given in this book (Chapter 6) from other countries are illustrations of this basic point.

The basic approach to national policies and programmes should be a public health perspective. This implies that primary prevention plays a key role, one of the fundamental tasks of information being to support policy

---

[a] Unpublished WHO document EB71/1983/REC/1, 1983.

[b] *Alcohol consumption and alcohol-related problems: development of national policies and programmes:* report on Technical Discussions (unpublished WHO document A35/Technical Discussions/6, 1982).

positions. Although treatment systems are important to national programmes, they cannot be the basic societal response to alcohol problems *(1)*. An attempt should be made to balance the view of the WHO Expert Committee *(4)* on the priority to be given to prevention, with the central argument of this chapter that any programme must include control, education and treatment. Although education has an autonomous position, its task is also to explain and support policy decisions. Of course, the balance between these activities and indeed the content of particular programmes are issues for national consideration.

The public health perspective implies that alcohol-related problems have to be considered in their totality, avoiding the pitfalls of concentrating exclusively on alcoholism, as a form of dependency or deviant behaviour *(5)*. The reference here to public health does not mean that all the consequences of drinking are primarily connected with public health since one could, for example, argue that public drunkenness is an issue of public order. As a basic approach, however, public health might be the most appropriate, especially since the point that alcoholism is likely to be a misleading rubric is now widely accepted.

Programmes have to relate the public health approach to the other interests involved, especially the economic ones. No programme can be effectively implemented without due consideration of "alcohol economics", the legitimate economic issues raised by a change in the relationship between alcohol and the state. This is one of the main conclusions from the report on the international study of alcohol control experiences *(5)* and the observations from other countries (see Chapter 6) illustrate that attention to economics has played an important part in the development of very different alcohol policies in Greece, Italy, Poland and Sweden.

Programmes should include discussion of strategies for stabilizing or lowering the level of consumption and for changing overall or specific drinking habits, as well as strategies concerning the particular types of alcohol-related problem that occur in the country concerned *(1,5)*. The balance between these elements is again a national issue, but it would be a great mistake to forget any of them. To include the level of consumption, drinking habits and types of alcohol problem means that it is possible to improve health by taking independent measures in each area, although activities in any one area may influence the others as well.

Data Base

Suitable models for describing historical developments and country profiles already exist and can be used *(3,6)*.

Although no country may be satisfied with the existing data as a basis for a programme, new extensive research is not usually necessary to develop a national policy. Instead, consultations with experts and knowledgeable citizens should be used as an expedient tool *(1)*.[a]

---

[a] Unpublished WHO document A35/Technical Discussions/1, 1982.

The request for an extensive data base and for extensive research before starting to develop national policies may often be quite unnecessary, especially since work on a policy document must be started before new data are needed. General statements about the need for research may, in fact, represent hidden resistance to a policy. Since there are many ways of collecting data, it should be recognized that too elaborate a research programme may be wasteful.

No country starts from scratch. Although alcohol may not be explicitly on the agenda, it will still be an object of fiscal or other types of control. An understanding of the basis for such measures gives a perspective for future policies *(3,5,6)*.

Despite the enormous variation among countries in the data available, every country can — with varying degrees of new data collection but without great expense — create a systematic description addressed to the following basic issues:

— identifying societal definitions of alcohol and alcohol problems;

— identifying major societal responses to alcohol and alcohol problems;

— identifying existing administrative responsibilities relevant to alcohol programmes;

— identifying perceptions of major alcohol problems;

— identifying possible neglected alcohol problems;

— identifying economic and other interests in the alcohol field, as well as organizations working in the area;

— giving at least crude estimates of alcohol consumption levels and descriptions of dominant drinking habits;

— identifying existing connections and commitments to international bodies (such as WHO or the Commission of the European Communities) that might have a bearing on the development of national policies and programmes *(3,5,6)*.

This list is really the core of this part of the discussion and can lead to some sort of formal protocol.

Towards a Policy

The first step in developing a national programme is to study the literature and develop the data base outlined above. In a sense, this is just a synthesis of the exercise described under the two previous headings. It is at this stage that it is especially worthwhile to relate possible national solutions to experiences drawn from the international literature.

If necessary, countries should at this stage consider consulting the programme and policy experiences of other countries that seem to have some relevance to the continuing development of their own national programme. Thus, explicit discussions could take place with representatives from other

140

relevant countries and it might be necessary to seek new data to be able to proceed. To introduce the question of new data at this late stage is intended to guarantee that there is a more precise idea about what data are needed.

Countries might also consider whether there are gaps in the data that necessitate further research. Research proposals should not, however, be used as an argument to postpone further policy programme development. Even when new data are needed, this should not require any interruption of the policy programme development, but rather the introduction of two parallel activities.

Once the data base has been developed, the systematic thinking that underpins it should be translated into a draft programme, consisting of at least the following elements:

— action to influence consumption levels and discussion of whether such action should be directed primarily to specific aspects of consumption (for instance, imported or locally produced brands, specific types of drink, duty-free alcohol, industrial alcohol, household production);

— action concerning specific types of alcohol use (such as at work);

— action concerning each important alcohol-related problem in the country concerned;

— action to improve administrative responsibilities and to divide them more explicitly if necessary;

— action to limit the economic interests that help increase the level of alcohol consumption or specific alcohol problems *(5,6)*.

This is in no sense a final or exclusive list, since proposed activities must relate to those that have already taken place in other countries. What is most important is to specify with as much detail as possible what should be done in each sector. On the question of administration it is important to observe that legal decisions have different impacts and that one key issue is the degree of loyalty within various parts of the administration *(5,6)*.

Having produced a programme outline, it should then be discussed and reformulated, taking a position on the following issues:

— at what political level the programme should be adopted;

— if adopted, how it should be explained, not only to those responsible for implementation, but also to a wider public;

— if adopted, how the information system and mass media could be involved in its implementation.

The Role of International Organizations

Consultative help could be provided to assist countries in their efforts to develop programmes.

Various international studies and reports on meetings may well be useful in creating insight into the need for a programme and in fostering a sympathetic international climate of opinion, but there will also be a need for concrete technical advice.

If international organizations provide consultants, guarantees of their continued assistance for at least five years may need to be given to the countries concerned. Only by means of such a commitment will historical and national variations be fully appreciated, so that the consultant can work effectively in close connection with a national group.

References

1. **Bruun, K. et al.** *Alcohol control policies in public health perspective.* Forssa, The Finnish Foundation for Alcohol Studies, 1975, Vol. 25.
2. *Public health aspects of alcohol and drug dependence:* report on a WHO Conference. Copenhagen, WHO Regional Office for Europe, 1979 (EURO Reports and Studies, No. 8).
3. **Moser, J.** *Prevention of alcohol-related problems. An international review of preventive measures, policies and programmes.* Toronto, Addiction Research Foundation, 1980.
4. WHO Technical Report Series, No. 650, 1980 (*Report of the WHO Expert Committee on Problems Related to Alcohol Consumption*).
5. **Mäkelä, K. et al.** *Alcohol, society, and the state. Vol. 1: a comparative study of alcohol control.* Toronto, Addiction Research Foundation, 1981.
6. **Single, E. et al., ed.** *Alcohol, society, and the state. Vol. 2: the social history of control policy in seven countries.* Toronto, Addiction Research Foundation, 1981.

9

National and international approaches: strengthening the links

M. Grant

Advocacy, Advice and Action

It is not, of course, the function of international bodies to tell countries what they must and must not do. This is as true in the area of alcohol policies as it is in any other. What they can do is to assemble previous relevant experience from countries that have, one way or another, attempted to introduce national alcohol policies. They can then draw up guidelines from those examples and, through appropriate advice and support, assist those countries that request it. It is important to recognize, however, that some countries may well choose not to develop policies at all and that others may choose to develop them without seeking advice from international organizations. In maintaining their ability to respond to a range of different requests from different countries, but mindful of the danger inherent in clinging to concepts that are rusting away through lack of use, international organizations can legitimately act in two ways. They can, through their advocacy role, encourage countries to develop their own national alcohol policies; and they can, in promoting appropriate technology, offer advice that will enable countries that do decide to act, to make their alcohol policies as effective as possible.

All that, however, presumes a serious and sustained commitment from the countries concerned. As Bruun points out in Chapter 8, and as is evident from the examples in Chapter 6 from Greece, Italy, Poland and Sweden, the development of national alcohol policies involves difficulties. It requires both imagination and a great deal of hard work. The delicate act of balancing economic interests and public health interests is perhaps the central obstacle, but it is certainly not the only one. Cooperation among many different interest groups, within and outside government, will be necessary. Ministries with responsibility for education, agriculture, trade, employment and social affairs, among others, will need to be involved. It may even be that the impetus to develop a national alcohol policy will stem from one of these ministries rather than from the ministry of health, although it is certain that the ministry of health will have to a play a very important part in its development. The ministry of finance cannot but be deeply involved in the implications of any suggested policy changes. Equally, however, interested bodies outside government will have a part to play. Treatment agencies, self-help organizations and other voluntary bodies, churches and teachers and parents organizations, will be likely to want to contribute to the process of policy development, and in some countries the list will be longer still. In addition, not only the alcoholic drinks industry but other industries, including catering, tourism, advertising and the media generally, will have essential contributions to make. The exclusion from the process of policy development of any significant interested party is likely to prejudice the subsequent successful implementation of the policy.

It would be naïve to suppose, however, that all the different interest groups will have compatible points of view. Even within government, there will be conflicts between some ministries, as well as agreements between others; nor will the areas of agreement or disagreement be the same in every country. Equally the policy, once developed, will not be immutable; as circumstances change so the policy will need to change with them, just as the existence of the policy will itself be likely to change a variety of contingent circumstances. The process of developing a national alcohol policy is therefore continuous, and does not imply a static position of any kind.

Within this complex interplay of different forces within countries, it is clear that the role of any international guidelines or advice is likely to be of importance in two distinct ways. Essential principles, such as the need to balance economic interests and public health interests, can be established; basic agendas can be drawn up for the area in which decisions have to be made; but the substance of these decisions is and will remain the prerogative of the countries themselves.

Linking National and International Efforts

While one of the main purposes of this book has been to distinguish between those issues to do with the development of alcohol policies that require action at the national level and those that require action at the international level, there are some important topics where links between national and international efforts are essential. The role of international organizations in terms of the assistance they can offer to countries that choose to develop their own policies has already been discussed. Four other topics, all of which have been touched upon by more than one author in this book, need to be mentioned in terms of the relative contributions they can make at national and international level to the formation of coherent plans for action.

Taxation
The first of these is taxation. Given the association between trends in alcohol consumption and trends in alcohol-related problems, it is clear that fiscal measures do have considerable potential from a public health perspective. Nevertheless, there are major differences between countries in the scope they offer for the use of taxation to modify consumption. Very high taxation levels can have unintended effects, including the encouragement of illicit

144

production and the consequent criminalization of large numbers of otherwise law-abiding citizens. Equally, the harmonization of taxation levels, such as is implied in the policies of the European Economic Community, can have the effect of reducing tax substantially in some countries, with likely consequent rises in consumption. These are questions that have to be considered from both a national and an international point of view, to achieve a reasonable balance between general political and economic considerations on the one hand and the public health aspects of alcohol availability on the other.

One further specific issue in the area of taxation requires coordinated international action, since no single country can act on it alone. The duty-free sale of alcohol to international travellers may be considered rather a marginal issue, but this is to fail to recognize its symbolic importance. It has special relevance from a European perspective, since a high proportion of such sales occur in connection with travel between countries in the European Region, especially in Scandinavia. Nevertheless, the principle is a global one and it can reasonably be argued that the practice of duty-free sales to travellers is neither logical in its own right nor compatible with the wider interests of public health.

Production and marketing

The second topic that needs to be considered from an international point of view, as well as nationally, is the production and marketing of alcoholic drinks. There are two strands to this question, one of which concerns the general upward trend in international trade associated with the growing influence of multinational corporations in the world alcohol marketplace. One aspect of this particular question of supply which is of special but not unique importance to countries in the European Region is the problem caused by the overproduction of wine. The second strand concerns marketing rather than production and focuses on the importance of alcohol advertising. Although the results of research into the effects of such advertising on aggregate consumption levels remain equivocal, it is clear that advertisements all carry cultural messages that are important in their own right. The diffusion of electronic media across national boundaries, a trend likely to be accelerated by means of satellite television broadcasting, requires that any steps taken to place restrictions on the content or frequency of such advertising should originate at an international level. At the same time, advertising restrictions by themselves are likely to be relatively futile unless they are in harmony with other aspects of the national alcohol policies of the countries concerned.

Health promotion

The third relevant topic is health promotion and it appears that the use of strategies from this area has been attracting increasing interest at national and international levels. It has been pointed out that health promotion can provide important support for other control measures and may indeed even be a prerequisite for their successful development and implementation. The relationship of health promotion to other aspects of national alcohol policies and the relationship of alcohol-specific health promotion activities to wider aspects of health, however, are both likely to remain problematic until the goals are clarified and made consistent with those of the alcohol policies, at the same time as being integrated with the wider health issues. Since this is an area of such considerable interest, to which high expectations are currently attached, it might be timely for a sustained effort to be made at an international level to encourage the appropriate evaluation of promising approaches, with a view to gathering and disseminating information on best practices.

Data collection

In support of these three topics, and in order to be able to come to more definite conclusions about the various trends in alcohol consumption and alcohol-related problems that are central to the development of national policies, real improvements in the collection of data are required. This is the final field where national and international efforts need to be closely linked. Countries that are not accustomed to gathering data on alcohol consumption and alcohol-related problems may need special help from the relevant international organizations. This could lead to an extension of valuable cross-national research initiatives to include countries previously under-represented in such studies. Even among those countries that already gather data on alcohol production and consumption and on alcohol-related mortality and morbidity, greater comparability remains an urgent requirement despite repeated resolutions of the World Health Assembly. So, too, does the encouragement of better time-series analyses of trends in alcohol-related problems. Developing countries, with scarce resources to devote to the compilation of data, may need guidance on which key indicators provide the most effective way of monitoring the impact of alcohol policy initiatives. Finally, in view of the increasing importance of an economic perspective, quantification of the health and social costs of alcohol consumption may require special attention.

Toasting Health for All by the Year 2000

This book began from the premise that the development of comprehensive national alcohol policies is the most effective way for countries to reduce the scale of alcohol-related problems. Working on the basis that the provision of examples from the past and guidelines for the future is likely to be of very considerable value to countries in their attempts to develop such policies, it has gone as far as present knowledge and expertise permits to provide such examples and guidelines. It needs to be emphasized, however, that this book is not the last word on the subject, but only the growing contribution to a continuing debate.

It also needs to be emphasized that the development of national alcohol policies is an activity for individual countries to undertake. This is not to deny international organizations a role in this area. It is probably true that national policies will stand or fall by the degree of international commitment to them that is forthcoming, in terms of advice and support. It is important to recognize that this involves a wide distribution of support. Even within WHO, it will involve contributions from major programme areas other than those traditionally associated with alcohol. Health education and health economics are two obvious examples, but there are others. Thus, beyond WHO, there are other agencies within the United Nations family that will also represent their own perspective in the provision of international support for this important effort. The public health perspective is vital to the process of helping countries develop effective alcohol policies, but it is not the only relevant perspective. It will not always be within ministries of health that the final touches will be put to national alcohol policies, which must after all, by definition, be comprehensive.

What is certain is that WHO can and must give a lead, both globally and regionally. It can give a lead through the coordination of international effort. It can give a lead through the active promotion of relevant concerns, both in its own programmes and in its relationship with Member States. Such a lead has been called for in the resolution of the World Health Assembly (WHA36.12) referred to at the beginning of this book. There is, in a real sense, no alternative. If WHO does not take this lead, then the world can look forward to further increases in alcohol consumption and to ever-mounting casualty rates from the awful battlefield of alcohol-related problems, until health for all by the year 2000 becomes a very hollow toast indeed.

PARTICIPANTS

Austria

Dr L. Wissgott, Mental Health Department, Federal Ministry of Health and Environmental Protection, Vienna

Belgium

Mr L. Bils, Director, Comité de Concertation sur l'Alcool et les autres Drogues, Brussels

Dr J. Casselman, Associate Professor in Mental Health, Catholic University of Leuven

Bulgaria

Dr M. Boyadjieva, Director, Department of Alcoholism and Drug Addiction, Sofia

Denmark

Mr T. Thorsen, Head of Section, Commission on Alcohol and Narcotics, Copenhagen

Finland

Mr U. Puustinen, Director, Department of Temperance and Alcohol, Ministry of Social Affairs and Health, Helsinki

France

Mrs M.T. Pierre, Sous-Directeur de la Maternité, de l'Enfance et des Actions spécifiques de Santé, Direction générale de la Santé, Ministère de la Santé, Paris

Mrs A. Georges, Médecin inspecteur de la Santé, Direction générale de la Santé, Ministère de la Santé, Paris

Mr H. Moyret, Président du Haut Comité d'Etude et d'Information sur l'Alcoolisme, Paris

Greece

Dr D. Yeroukalis, Clinic for Alcohol and Drug Abuse, National Hospital for Mental Diseases, Dafni–Attiki, Athens

Hungary

Dr M. Bonta, Chairman of the Hungarian National Committee against Alcoholism, Budapest

Iceland

Mr H. Palsson, Consultant, Ministry for Health and Social Security, Reykjavik

Dr S. Sigfusson, Department of Psychiatry, Landspitallin, Reykjavik

Luxembourg

Mr P. Neuberg, Centre thérapeutique d'Useldange, Hôpital neuropsychiatrique de l'Etat, Ettelbruck

Norway

Dr O. Aasland, Medical Director, Statens Edrupskapsdirektorat, Oslo

Poland

Professor I. Wald, Psychoneurological Institute, Warsaw

Portugal

Dr M.L. Mercês de Mello, Director, Centro de Recuperação de Alcoólicos, Hospital Sobral Cid, Coimbra

Spain

Dr R. Enriquez de Salamanca, Head of the Unit of Alcohol and Drug Addiction, General Directorate of Public Health, Ministry of Health and Consumer Affairs, Madrid

Sweden

Mr J. Lindberg, Director, Division for Social Services, Ministry of Health and Social Services, Stockholm

Switzerland

Dr C. Zurbrügg, Sous-directeur, Régie fédérale des Alcools, Berne

United Kingdom

Dr R. Wawman, Senior Medical Officer, Department of Health and Social Security, London

Yugoslavia

Dr I. Tulevski, Chief, Department of Epidemiology and Statistics, Clinic for Neurological and Psychiatric Disorders, Skopje

Representatives of other organizations

Commission of the European Communities (CEC)

Dr L.R. Karhausen, Directorate for Health and Safety, Luxembourg–Kirchberg, Luxembourg

Council of Europe

Mrs V. Marsarelli Boltho, Division de la Santé, Strasbourg, France

International Commission for the Prevention of Alcoholism (ICPA)

Dr W. Beaven, Kettering College of Medical Arts, Kettering, OH, USA

International Council on Alcohol and Addictions (ICAA)

Mr A. Tongue, Executive Director, Lausanne, Switzerland

Dr P. Schioler, Chief Adviser to the Danish Ministry of Education on Alcohol and Narcotic Problems, Ministry of Education, Copenhagen, Denmark

Nordic Council

Dr O.J. Skog, National Institute for Alcohol Research, Oslo, Norway

*United Nations Educational, Scientific and Cultural Organization
(UNESCO)*

Mrs N. Friderich, Chief, Section of Education concerning the Problems
associated with the Use of Drugs, Paris, France

Observers

Mr H. Bazin, Directeur de la Fédération internationale des Vins et
Spiritueux, Paris, France

Mr J.-J. Bouffard, Institut de Recherche et des Etudes des Boissons,
Paris, France

Mr J. Serignan, Président du Comité national de Défense contre l'Alcoolisme, Paris, France

Consultant

Mr M. Grant, Alcohol Education Centre, Institute of Psychiatry, London, United Kingdom

Temporary advisers

Dr K.E. Bruun, Institute of Sociology, Stockholm University, Sweden

Professor A. Cottino, Faculty of Political Science, University of Turin,
Italy

Mr M.J. van Iwaarden, 2nd Secretary of the Interdepartmental Steering
Group on Alcohol and Drug Policies (ISAD), Ministry of Welfare,
Health and Cultural Affairs, Leidschendam, Netherlands

Dr K. Mäkelä, Research Director, The Finnish Foundation for Alcohol
Studies, Helsinki, Finland

Dr R.G.W. Room, Scientific Director, Social Research Group, School
of Public Health, University of California, Berkeley, CA, USA

Dr I. Rootman, Chief, Health Promotion Studies Unit, Health Promotion Directorate, Ottawa, Canada

Professor R. Senault, Président de l'Office d'Hygiène sociale de
Meurthe-et-Moselle, Vandœuvre, France

Dr P. Sulkunen, The Finnish Foundation for Alcohol Studies, Helsinki, Finland

Professor B. Walsh, Department of Economics, University College, Belfield, Dublin, Ireland

Dr J. Yfantopoulos, Health Economist, Ministry of Health and Welfare, Athens, Greece

World Health Organization

Regional Office for Europe

Mr J.U. Hannibal, Technical Officer for Mental Health

Dr J.H. Henderson, Regional Officer for Mental Health

Headquarters

Mr J. Ording, Senior Scientist, Division of Mental Health